917.95 St
Stein, R. Conard
America the beautiful - Oregon

AMERICA the BEAUTIFUL

OREGON

By R. Conrad Stein

Consultants

Gordon B. Dodds, Ph.D., Professor of History, Portland State University

Marjorie A. Covey, Director, Instructional Materials and Resources Center, Marion Education Service District, Salem

Robert L. Hillerich, Ph.D., Bowling Green State University

CHILDRENS PRESS®

CHICAGO

The Old Columbia River Highway near Hood River

Project Editor: Joan Downing
Associate Editor: Shari Joffe
Design Director: Margrit Fiddle
Typesetting: Graphic Connections, Inc.
Engraving: Liberty Photoengraving

Library of Congress Cataloging-in-Publication Data

Stein, R. Conrad.
   America the beautiful. Oregon / by R. Conrad Stein.
      p.   cm.
   Includes index.
   Summary: Introduces the geography, history,
government, economy, industry, culture, historic
sites, and famous people of the state known as the
"Pacific Wonderland."
   ISBN 0-516-00384-2
   1. Oregon—Juvenile literature.
[1. Oregon] I. Title.
F876.3.S74 1989   88-38528
979.5—dc19   CIP
                                           AC

The Portland skyline and the Willamette River

TABLE OF CONTENTS

Chapter 1
WELCOME TO OREGON

WELCOME TO OREGON

A writer once asked an Oregonian to describe his state.

"Describe Oregon . . . ," the Oregonian said thoughtfully. "Describe Oregon . . ." Then he shrugged his shoulders, looked at the writer, and said, "Which Oregon do you mean?"

Oregon is a land too diverse to capture in a single description. It encompasses, in fact, many lands. In Oregon rise lofty mountain peaks that are snow-covered even in July, and lush, almost tropical valleys where flowers bloom year-round. The state has forests so thick that the sun barely penetrates them, while just a short drive away spreads a sun-drenched desert dotted with lonely sagebrush.

The mountain ranges that stand near Oregon's coast have greatly influenced the state. These majestic guardians affect the state's climate, its vegetation, and its reputation.

Oregon was settled by a hearty breed of pioneers who risked their lives to cross the continent in covered wagons. Early in the twentieth century, Oregon was the spawning ground for a new political movement that sought to take decision-making powers away from government bureaucrats and give them back to the citizens.

"Welcome to Oregon" say signs along the state's borders. Oregon boasts warm and energetic people and a glorious, adventure-filled history. Its towns harbor museums, theaters, and architectural surprises. Its countryside is so breathtaking that Oregon is often called the Pacific Wonderland.

Chapter 2
THE LAND

THE LAND

Oregon is a Pacific Northwest state. Roughly rectangular in shape, it is bordered by California and Nevada on the south, Idaho on the east, and Washington on the north. The long and rugged Pacific coastline determines the state's western boundary.

Spreading over 97,073 square miles (251,419 square kilometers), Oregon is the tenth-largest American state. Its greatest distance from east to west is 401 miles (645 kilometers); its greatest distance from north to south is 294 miles (473 kilometers).

Salem is Oregon's capital, and Portland is the state's largest city.

A LAND OF FANTASTIC VARIETY

A trip across the width of Oregon, from the Pacific coast to the Idaho border, offers dramatic changes for the traveler. As one travels eastward, the ocean's pounding surf fades away as gentle mountains covered with ferns come into view. In northern Oregon, the traveler then descends into the rich, green Willamette Valley. After the valley, the land surges skyward. Here are mountains where pines and firs stand like brooding giants and where snow covers the ground even in summer. Then, with breathtaking suddenness, the land changes again—into a flatter land, deeply cut by river canyons and dotted with sagebrush and even cactus. Farther northeast, another forested, mountainous

Mount Hood is Oregon's tallest peak.

region appears. Finally, at the Idaho border, the trip ends in the exciting Snake River country.

Oregon's incredible shifts in scenery are created by its mountain ranges, which divide the state into two distinct regions. The western one-third of the state is moist and forested; the eastern two-thirds is generally drier and flatter. The dividing line is formed by the Cascade Mountains. The Cascades include some of the nation's tallest mountains. Mount Hood, Oregon's tallest peak, rises 11,239 feet (3,426 meters) in the heart of the Cascades. West of the Cascades stand the Klamath Mountains and the Coast

Top left: Aspens and ponderosa pines in Willamette National Forest
Bottom left: South Sister Mountain in the Three Sisters Wilderness

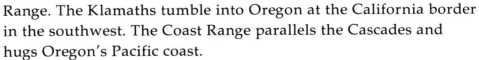

Range. The Klamaths tumble into Oregon at the California border in the southwest. The Coast Range parallels the Cascades and hugs Oregon's Pacific coast.

Many of Oregon's mountains are actually inactive volcanoes. In 1980, Oregonians were brutally reminded of the unstable nature of volcanoes. That year, Mount St. Helens in neighboring Washington erupted, killing thirty-six people, leaving twenty-one

Top left: Mount Jefferson and the Mount Jefferson Wilderness Area
Bottom left: Wahkeena Creek and wildflowers along the Old Columbia River Highway
Bottom right: A blueberry farm near Sandy

missing, and scattering volcanic ash over Portland and other parts of Oregon.

In northwest Oregon, tucked between the Coast Range and the Cascades, is the Willamette Valley. About 180 miles (290 kilometers) long and 60 miles (97 kilometers) wide, the Willamette Valley is the historical heart and soul of Oregon. The valley contains the state's richest farmland, the greatest

13

Right: Smith Rock State Park in central Oregon
Bottom left: Rock formations in Leslie Gulch
in southeastern Oregon
Bottom right: Rolling farmland near The Dalles
in north-central Oregon

concentration of industry, and more than half of Oregon's
population.

From the Cascades east to the Idaho border spreads a drier
region. Geologically, this portion of the state is known as the
Columbia Plateau. Much of this region is "high desert," a type of
land found in arid regions that lie between 4,000 and 7,500 feet

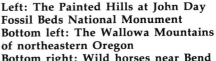

Left: The Painted Hills at John Day
Fossil Beds National Monument
Bottom left: The Wallowa Mountains
of northeastern Oregon
Bottom right: Wild horses near Bend
in central Oregon

(between 1,219 and 2,286 meters) above sea level. In the state's
northeast corner, rolling forests blanket the Blue and Wallowa
mountains. Along the Idaho border, the Snake River has carved
out Hells Canyon, a fantastic gorge that is deeper than the Grand
Canyon. Southeastern Oregon, much of which is semidesert, is
part of the Basin and Range Region, which extends into California
and other nearby states.

15

Oneonta Gorge
in the Columbia
River Gorge

RIVERS, LAKES, AND SEACOAST

The Columbia River forms most of the border between Oregon
and Washington as it flows westward to empty into the Pacific
Ocean. Throughout history, the mighty Columbia has been the
Pacific Northwest's most important river. It drains the northern
half of Oregon and allows the inland city of Portland to serve as
an ocean port. The Columbia was key to the exploration and
settlement of the area. The Columbia River Gorge along the river
is one of the scenic wonders of North America.

Major tributaries of the Columbia are the Willamette River, the
Deschutes River, the John Day River, Rock Creek, Willow Creek,
and the Umatilla River. In eastern Oregon, the wild and beautiful
Snake River makes up much of the state's border with Idaho.
Snake River tributaries include the Imnaha, Powder, Burnt,
Malheur, and Owyhee rivers. The Rogue River, the Sprague River,
and Silver Creek lie in the south. The Rogue cuts through a
spectacular wilderness valley and is especially appreciated by
hikers and white-water rafters.

Among Oregon's hundreds of waterfalls are Horsetail Falls in the Columbia River Gorge (left) and Proxy Falls in the Three Sisters Wilderness (above).

Oregon's maze of rivers and towering mountains give the state many glorious waterfalls. Some are mere trickles, while others tumble off cliffs higher than a three-story building. Notable waterfalls include Benham, Silver Creek, Bridal Veil, Horsetail, and Multnomah.

Oregon has more than six thousand lakes, ranging from forest ponds to reservoirs covering more than 1,000 acres (405 hectares). Crater Lake, in southern Oregon, was formed thousands of years ago when water collected in the mouth of an extinct volcano. Nearly 2,000 feet (610 meters) in depth, Crater Lake is the nation's deepest lake. Waldo Lake, Diamond Lake, and Howard Prairie Reservoir are major lakes in the Cascade Mountains. Upper Klamath Lake is the state's largest lake. In the dry southeast spread the shallow Harney and Malheur lakes.

Counting bays and peninsulas, Oregon has about 400 miles (644 kilometers) of Pacific coastline. The Oregon coastline is a series of rugged, rocky cliffs, a world apart from the gentle beaches of

Left: The coastline at Seal Rock
Above: The rocks at Cannon Beach
known as The Needles

southern California. Over the centuries, waves and windblown
sand have sculpted enormous offshore rocks into odd shapes,
prompting such names as Haystack Rock, Seal Rock, and Otter
Rock. With the exception of the most sheltered bays, water along
the coast is icy cold even in the summer months. So instead of
taking a swim, most visitors satisfy themselves with long,
thoughtful walks along the windswept beaches.

CLIMATE

Portland and the Willamette Valley are famed—and sometimes
cursed—for their foggy, misty winters. The season-long cloud
cover seems to bring on a condition that some natives call the
"Oregon blues." Yet a short drive away, in central Oregon, skies
are cloudless and rain is rare. Oregon's mountainous "spine" in

Right: Fog along the coast near Port Orford

the western third of the state is partly responsible for this phenomenon. Warm, moist winds sweep in from the Pacific coast. As they travel east, the winds are deflected upward off the Coast Range and the Cascades. As the warm air rises, it cools, the moisture condenses, and rain falls—on the western side of the mountains. The eastern part of the state remains relatively dry.

Aside from the winter fog, the Oregon coast and the Willamette Valley enjoy a pleasant climate, as the heavy, wet air protects the land from extreme seasonal changes. From May through October, the western third of Oregon is blessed with sunshine and warm breezes. The average temperature along the coast is 45 degrees Fahrenheit (7 degrees Celsius) in January and 60 degrees Fahrenheit (15.5 degrees Celsius) in July. Farmers in the Willamette Valley enjoy a growing season of 250 days.

Beyond the Cascades, the dry air of the eastern two-thirds of Oregon leaves the land open to sharp seasonal changes. In central

Oregon's varied terrain includes tidepools
carpeted with sea life and lush woodlands
blanketed with wildflowers and wild plants.

Oregon, winter frosts reduce the growing season to 125 days or
less. The highest and lowest temperatures recorded in the state
both occurred on the eastern plains. In February 1933, the
temperature dropped to minus 54 degrees Fahrenheit (minus 48
degrees Celsius) at Ukiah and Seneca. In the summer of 1898, the
mercury rose to a scorching 119 degrees Fahrenheit (48 degrees
Celsius) at Prineville and Pendleton.

PLANT AND ANIMAL LIFE

Forests cover about half of Oregon. Although Oregon has
thirteen national forests, most of the forests are commercial
forestland. For many years, wood processing has been the state's

leading industry. About one-tenth of the nation's timber supply comes from Oregon. The Douglas fir, the state tree, is the most commercially important tree in Oregon. Hemlocks, cedars, pines, and spruces are important softwood trees that grow in the state. Hardwoods include cottonwoods, junipers, maples, and willows.

Wildflowers blanket the ground in the dry as well as the wet regions. Saddle Mountain, in the Coast Range, is graced with two thousand species of wildflowers. Some, such as the moccasin flower, are rare. Others, such as buttercups and Indian pipes, are common. The Oregon grape, the state flower, grows in most parts of the state.

The beaver, Oregon's state animal, has also given the state its nickname: the Beaver State. Oregon beavers were once trapped almost to extinction, but strict conservation laws enacted in the early 1900s helped the population renew itself. In the state's forests live deer, elk, black bears, bobcats, foxes, mountain goats, minks, coyotes, and river otters. Bighorn sheep roam the Cascades, and pronghorn antelope graze on the eastern plains. Songbirds perform their magic throughout the state. One of the sweetest voices is the western meadowlark, the Oregon state bird. Other birds found in Oregon include cormorants, cranes, pelicans, geese, and gulls.

Oregon's coastal waters, rivers, and lakes are rich with life. Seals and sea lions bark and bask along huge rocks on the coast. People hiking along the oceanside cliffs sometimes see whales bobbing their way through the waves. The state's freshwater fish include perch, striped bass, sturgeon, and steelhead trout. During the spawning season, salmon (the state fish) struggle up streams to lay their eggs. Hundreds of years ago, the Northwest Indians believed that the gods commanded the salmon to swim against the current, thus making the tasty fish easier to catch.

Chapter 3
THE
PEOPLE

THE PEOPLE

*Oregon is a diverse state, and our citizens
represent many cultures and values. Enjoy it. . . .*
—from a 1988 address by Oregon Governor Neil Goldschmidt

POPULATION AND POPULATION DISTRIBUTION

Oregon had a population of 2,633,149 according to the 1980
census. The number represented a whopping 26 percent increase
over the 1970 figure. An estimate in 1988 put the state's
population at 2,741,000, indicating that the state's growth was less
rapid in the 1980s than it had been in the 1970s. Oregon ranks
thirtieth in population among the states.

Oregon is an uncrowded state. Its population density averages
only 28 people per square mile (11 people per square kilometer).
By contrast, the national average is 67 people per square mile (26
people per square kilometer).

The rich Willamette Valley is home to the greatest concentration
of Oregonians. In order of population (according to the 1980
census), the state's largest cities are Portland, Eugene, Salem,
Springfield, Corvallis, and Medford. All these cities, except
Medford, lie in the Willamette Valley. About 40 percent of the
state's people live in the Portland area.

Eastern Oregon is much less populated. In fact, the eastern two-
thirds of the land contains only 12 percent of the people. The
population density of Harney County, in the southeast, averages
less than 1 person per square mile (.4 persons per square
kilometer).

Portland is Oregon's most-populous city.

Although Oregon is sparsely populated, its population is mainly urban. About six out of ten Oregonians live in cities and towns. Yet, aside from Portland, the state's cities tend to be small. Portland's population approaches 370,000, while Eugene and Salem are the only other Oregon cities that claim more than 50,000 people.

WHO ARE THE OREGONIANS?

During the pioneer era of the 1800s, Oregon was settled largely by hardy midwesterners. A steady stream of migrants, most of whom were white Americans, followed the early pioneers. World War I and World War II brought thousands of industrial workers to the state. In the 1960s and 1970s, many young Americans came to Oregon to take advantage of the state's unspoiled wilderness areas.

Today, 96 percent of Oregon's people are native-born Americans. About 95 percent of the population is white, 2 percent is of Hispanic origin, 1 percent is black, 1 percent is Asian, and 1 percent is Native American (American Indian). While the state's thirty thousand Indians live throughout the state, some choose to reside on reservation lands. Oregon has four Indian reservations. The largest is Warm Springs, which lies east of the Cascade Mountains near the town of Warm Springs.

RELIGION

Methodist missionaries played a vital role in Oregon's settlement by whites, and early in the state's history, Methodism was the dominant religion of the population. Today, Oregon remains overwhelmingly Protestant. The Methodist, Mormon, Presbyterian, Lutheran, and Episcopalian churches are among the most widely followed Protestant denominations. Catholics make up the state's largest single Christian group. A Jewish congregation was established in Portland as early as 1858, and today the state has a small Jewish population. Islam and other eastern religions are becoming more widespread in the state.

The freedom provided by Oregon's untamed wilderness has long attracted people who wished to gather and form religious communities. One of the early communes was led by William Keil. In the mid-1800s, Keil led some five hundred German-Dutch followers from Bethel, Missouri, to the Aurora Colony. Usually, the religious societies lived in peace with other Oregonians. A recent exception was a commune in rural Oregon that was founded in 1981 by the Bhagwan Shree Rajneesh. Commune members bought a huge ranch and gave their leader a fleet of ninety Rolls Royce automobiles. The group outraged people of Wasco County when they brought in people to vote in a local election in an attempt to outnumber the legitimate Wasco County voters. The commune collapsed in 1985, when the federal government deported the Bhagwan Shree Rajneesh to India because of immigration irregularities.

POLITICAL ISSUES AND POLITICAL MAVERICKS

Protecting the environment is perhaps the state's most hotly debated issue. Battle lines on environmental issues are often drawn between aesthetics and economics. For example, many newcomers, who came to Oregon to enjoy its beauty, insist the forests be left alone. In contrast, many longtime Oregonians hold jobs in the timber industry and favor laws allowing lumber companies to cut at least a limited number of trees.

Over the years, pro-conservation forces have won important political victories in Oregon. Today, Oregon manages more than 785,000 acres (317,682 hectares) of state forestland where commercial harvesting of trees is a strictly controlled activity. Oregon has also acquired 223 state park areas that total 88,267 acres (35,721 hectares) of land. Reserved entirely for public use, the state parks are off-limits to development by private industry.

Oregonians have long been familiar with political leaders who delight in writing their own rules. Wayne Morse was the state's most famous political maverick. In the 1940s, Morse served in the United States Senate as a Republican. He became an Independent in 1952, and finally switched to the Democratic party in 1955. In the early 1960s, Morse was one of the few senators to speak out against the Vietnam War. Governor and later Senator Mark Hatfield was another outspoken opponent of American involvement in Vietnam. As a young serviceman, Hatfield saw the ruins of Hiroshima, and the experience made him a lifelong peace advocate. Tom McCall, governor of the state from 1967 to 1975, advocated public ownership of the coast and showed concern for other ecological issues. At the end of his second term as governor, he became seriously ill, yet he stayed in office even though the stress of the job aggravated his illness.

Chapter 4
THE BEGINNINGS

THE BEGINNINGS

In the beginning, only animals dwelled in the mountains and forests. An evil monster lurked in the hills, and all the forest creatures lived in fear of him. Then Coyote—the most powerful and cleverest of all spirits—slew the monster and scattered its blood across the rocky land that lies east of the Cascades. From each drop of the monster's blood sprang a man or a woman.
—Nez Percé creation myth

THE FIRST OREGONIANS

An ancient landmark known as Fort Rock lies in a harsh climate east of the Cascades. It was at this isolated spot that an archaeological team discovered seventy sandals made from woven cord and sagebrush bark. The find was so remarkable that the team called it the "shoe store." Tests determined that the sandals and other materials found in the area dated from 9000-13,000 B.C. Human remains unearthed from graves at the site indicate that most of these early people died before reaching the age of twenty.

Fort Rock was the site of one of the earliest human settlements ever found in Oregon. The Fort Rock people were descendants of the original Americans; hardy men and women who migrated to North America from Asia twenty thousand to forty thousand years ago.

Unlike the Mound Builders to the east and the Anasazi to the south, the ancient people of the Pacific Northwest left behind no cities or huge temples. Consequently, little is known about prehistoric Oregon society. We do know that these early Oregonians were inspired to create art. On a Fort Rock cave wall, archaeologists found a fading picture of a hunter poised to throw a spear. More is known about the people who lived during the "contact period" after about A.D. 1500, when Indian people first encountered whites.

LIFE DURING THE CONTACT PERIOD

At the time of the arrival of the first white settlers, the land of present-day Oregon had about one hundred tribes that spoke dialects of twelve different languages. The population was perhaps thirty-eight thousand. Five tribes—the Klamaths, the Modocs, the Paiutes, the Nez Percé, and the Chinooks—dominated the regions where they lived.

The Klamaths and Modocs (two closely related peoples) lived in the Klamath Mountains and along the shores of Lake Klamath. They were sometimes called the "pit Indians" because their houses were dugout pits roofed by branches, grass, and tree bark. Their homeland was a marshy area dotted by lakes and ponds. Waterfowl, fish, and seeds were their staple foods. The most powerful member of their society was the high priest, or shaman, who interpreted signs in the sky to foretell future events.

East of the Klamath Mountains lived the Paiutes. Their beautiful but rain-starved land produced little to eat, and in order to survive, the Paiutes were often forced to eat mice, roots, and insects. Their hunger was sated only at certain times of the year, when various Paiute tribes banded together to herd and capture jackrabbits.

Northeast Oregon was the territory of the prosperous Nez Percé people. The Nez Percé were merchants and warriors. Long before

Fish was an essential part of the diet of the Indians who lived along the Columbia River. This painting shows salmon drying on racks in a Nez Percé village.

the white man came to the region, the Nez Percé had acquired his most precious servant—the horse. In the early 1700s, Nez Percé trading parties brought horses from the American Southwest to their Pacific Northwest homelands. The Nez Percé were the first American Indian people to practice selective breeding, and they produced strong, swift animals.

The Chinooks lived along the Pacific coast near the mouth of the Columbia River. Fish was their staple food, and they lent their name to one of the Northwest's most important game fish—the chinook salmon. Chinook men were renowned for their courage and skill; they were expert at handling their elaborately carved cedar canoes on the stormy ocean and on the swift rivers. To celebrate an important event such as a royal marriage, the Chinooks held a great feast called a potlatch. During a potlatch, the host was required to demonstrate his generosity by giving away nearly all his possessions to the dinner guests.

The Indians of the Pacific Northwest wove grasses into beautiful, sturdy baskets.

The Indians of the Northwest found ingenious ways to use Oregon's wealth of trees and plants. Along the coast, cedar trees were fashioned into canoes or used to make large communal houses. Grasses were woven into tough baskets. Bows were made of flexible but strong crab-apple wood. The roots of the wild poppy were used to treat toothache pain. A tea made from dogwood bark was said to ease the suffering of colds and flu. Skin diseases were treated with a paste made from the scarlet sumac.

Then, as now, the people had to cope with the sharp divisions of land created by Oregon's mountains. Excellent fishing existed along the coast, while good hunting usually prevailed in the forests. Because of the area's bountiful natural resources, the people of the Northwest Coast were among the most affluent of all North American Indians. The peoples who lived in the Willamette Valley, along the Columbia River, and in the Snake River country also found abundant fish and good hunting. However, the peoples of Oregon's rainless southeast did not enjoy such an abundance of food and always had to struggle to survive.

The lives of Oregon's Indians were deeply affected by religion. Religious practices differed widely from tribe to tribe, but the various groups held certain convictions and rituals in common. The belief in a great creator—usually represented by the coyote—was common in nearly all the tribes of the Pacific Northwest. In addition to the coyote, there were hundreds of lesser spirits that could work good or mischief to mankind. In Indian society, nothing happened by chance. If a person fell into a lake and drowned, that incident was thought of as the work of an evil spirit. Oregon Indians believed that after death, the soul departs from the body and rises to a marvelous spirit world.

THE EXPLORERS

The first known Europeans to spot the shores of Oregon were Spanish seamen aboard a ship commanded by Lieutenant Bartolomé Ferrelo in the 1540s. The Spaniards were probing the Pacific Northwest in hopes of discovering a waterway leading from the Pacific Ocean eastward across the North American continent. About forty years later, Englishman Sir Francis Drake, also seeking a water route through America, sailed along the Oregon coast. A "Northwest Passage," as European sea captains envisioned it, did not exist. However, the early explorers did miss a significant waterway. The Columbia River offers a water route of more than 200 miles (322 kilometers) inland from the Pacific Ocean. But despite the efforts of explorers, the Columbia River—the major waterway of the Pacific Northwest—went undiscovered for two more centuries.

The mighty Columbia was finally found and traveled by a gifted Rhode Island-born sea captain named Robert Gray. Gray was the first American captain to take a ship completely around the world.

On his second expedition to the Oregon region, in 1792, Gray's curiosity led him to examine a huge opening in the Pacific coastal rocks. His vessel was dashed about by treacherous currents, but using all his skill, Gray inched his ship into a broad river that had never before been seen by whites. He called the river *Columbia*, after his ship. For years, however, certain Indians of the Northwest had called the river *Ouragon*, *Origan*, or *Oregon*. Europeans and Americans later referred to the area surrounding the great river as the Oregon country, or simply Oregon.

A more deliberate exploration of Oregon came not by sea, but by a heroic overland expedition. "The object of your mission," said the written orders from President Thomas Jefferson to Meriwether Lewis and William Clark, "is to explore the Missouri River and [discover] the most direct and practical water communication across this continent. . . ." Heeding these orders, the forty-five men of the Lewis and Clark Expedition left St. Louis in 1804 and plunged into the unknown lands of the American West. Their destination was the Pacific Ocean—nearly 3,000 miles (4,828 kilometers) away.

In keelboats and canoes, riding horseback and trudging on foot, the party pushed steadily into the wilderness. After eighteen months of rugged traveling, Lewis and Clark crossed the Snake River and entered present-day Oregon. There they met the Nez Percé people. Clark, admiring the beautiful Columbia River Gorge, wrote in his journal, "This is certainly a fertile and handsome valley, at this time crowded with Indians." In November 1805, near present-day Astoria, the men spotted the gleaming Pacific Ocean. Meriwether Lewis wrote, "We enjoyed the delightful prospect of the ocean—that ocean, the object of all our labors, the reward of all our anxieties."

The Lewis and Clark Expedition accomplished many goals for

Astoria, founded in 1811, was the first permanent white settlement in the Oregon country.

the United States. It—and the Gray Expedition a dozen years earlier—gave the nation a strong political claim to the Oregon country. These expeditions also made the Pacific Northwest seem less remote in the minds of Americans. Furthermore, Lewis and Clark brought back reports that the region was rich in beavers and other fur-bearing animals. In the early 1800s, furs were literally worth their weight in gold in Europe.

FUR AND POLITICS

In 1811, a group of men employed by American businessman John Jacob Astor established a fur-trading post, called Astoria, at the mouth of the Columbia River. At first, the men of Astoria were in fine spirits. A company clerk wrote, "The weather was magnificent, and all nature smiled. The forests looked like pleasant groves, and the leaves like flowers." However, the

John McLoughlin (inset), known as the Father of Oregon, directed the activities of the Hudson's Bay Company from Fort Vancouver (above).

company soon lost their ship and several men in clashes with the Indians. In addition, the Americans faced competition from the British-owned North West Company, which had been established north of the Columbia River. When the War of 1812 broke out between the United States and England, the American fur traders were forced to sell the post at Astoria to the North West Company.

In 1821, the British government gave the Hudson's Bay Company, which had merged with the North West Company, a monopoly over fur trade in the Pacific Northwest. In charge of the company's Oregon interests was the remarkable Canadian-born John McLoughlin. Under McLoughlin's leadership, Fort Vancouver (present-day Vancouver, Washington) was built on the northern bank of the Columbia just above the mouth of the Willamette. For the next two decades, the fort served as a wilderness metropolis for the vast Oregon country. McLoughlin directed the company's activities and ruled the region as if it were his private kingdom.

Though the fur trade brought profits to the Hudson's Bay Company, it spelled disaster for Oregon's Indians. The Indians could obtain such goods as iron pots and fishhooks only by trading beaver pelts with the whites. Soon, many Indians abandoned their age-old practice of working as independent hunters and became trappers for the Hudson's Bay Company. Worse yet, the white traders brought to Oregon deadly diseases such as smallpox and diphtheria. The Native Americans had no natural immunities to these illnesses, and devastating epidemics swept through their villages. By 1846, the Indian population had been reduced by two-thirds, leaving perhaps twelve thousand Indians in the Oregon region.

Because of its profitable fur trade, the Oregon country became entangled in international politics. The region had no official boundaries. The land that was called Oregon ranged roughly from Alaska to California and from the Rocky Mountains to the Pacific shore. This immense, fur-rich territory was coveted by Russia, Spain, England, and Oregon's continental neighbor—the United States. In 1818 and again in 1827, the United States and England agreed that both countries would trade and settle the region. Spain was gradually losing its overseas empire and, in a treaty that established Oregon's southern border, dropped its claims to Oregon in 1819. Five years later, the Russians also surrendered their holdings in the region. Oregon's destiny thus became a contest between the old and the new, the mother and the son— Great Britain and the United States.

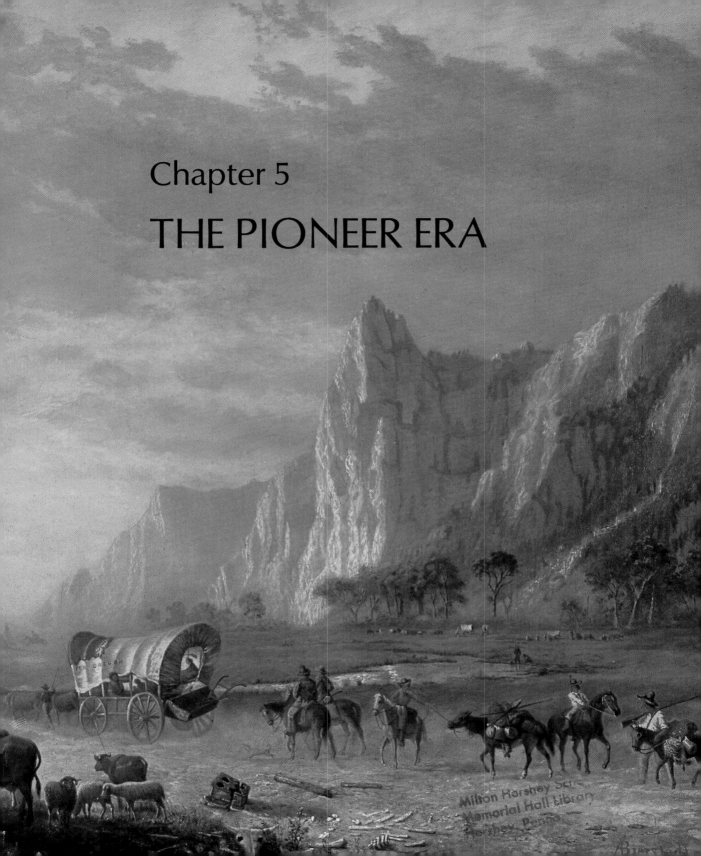

Chapter 5
THE PIONEER ERA

THE PIONEER ERA

*Eastward I go only by force, but westward
I go free . . . this is the prevailing tendency of
my countrymen. I must walk toward Oregon. . . .*
—American writer Henry David Thoreau

OREGON DREAMING

Though it was an isolated, undeveloped region, Oregon lived in
the dreams of a handful of idealistic Americans. One was Boston
schoolteacher Hall Jackson Kelley, who had studied the journals
of Lewis and Clark. Kelley formed a society urging New
Englanders to journey to Oregon and establish American
communities there. Fellow New Englander Nathaniel Wyeth
followed Kelley's advice and made two trips to Oregon in the
1830s. Accompanying Wyeth on his second journey were
Methodist ministers Jason and Daniel Lee. They were the first of a
number of Protestant clergymen who traveled to Oregon to bring
Christianity to the Indians.

A remarkable party of missionaries, headed by Marcus
Whitman and his wife Narcissa, made the arduous overland
journey from New York to the Oregon country in 1836. Mrs.
Whitman kept a diary of her experiences on the trail. While
traveling over the scorching Great Plains, she wrote, "Truly I
thought the heavens over us were brass, and the earth iron under
our feet." The beauty of the Rocky Mountains overwhelmed her,

but she deplored the tortuous pathway. "[The path] was like winding stairs . . . and in some places almost perpendicular."

Mrs. Whitman and the wife of another missionary were the first white women to cross the continent over what became known as the Oregon Trail. That trail began at Independence, Missouri, and wound some 2,000 miles (3,219 kilometers) to the Pacific Northwest.

By the beginning of the 1840s, seven American-run missions were operating in the Oregon country. The Methodists founded a school (the forerunner of today's Willamette University) in the Willamette Valley in 1842. In 1843, the first large overland migration—about a thousand people—traveled the Oregon Trail. That same year, about one hundred American and French-Canadian settlers met in the tiny town of Champoeg to establish a rudimentary government.

As head of the British-owned Hudson's Bay Company, John McLoughlin was supposed to discourage American settlement in the Oregon country. Instead, he gave the newly arriving farmers and missionaries food, money, and advice. It simply was against his character to force people off the land. He did, however, try to insist that American settlements be kept south of the Columbia River. When McLoughlin retired from the company, he became an American citizen, and today he is regarded as the Father of Oregon.

OREGON BECOMES AMERICAN

For decades, American and British diplomats argued over the status of the huge Oregon country. With more and more American settlers pouring in, it seemed clear that the British would eventually have to give up the region. In 1844, James K.

Polk ran for president of the United States under the slogan "Fifty-four Forty or Fight!" Polk and his backers demanded that the British relinquish their claim to all the land south of 54°40', a boundary that lies near present-day Alaska. Slogans and threats aside, the United States and Great Britain agreed peacefully on a compromise treaty in 1846. Britain surrendered its claim on the Oregon territory that lay south of the 49° line. This line still stands as the border between the United States and Canada. At the time of the agreement, more than two thousand Americans were living in the Willamette Valley, and more were arriving every year.

While the border agreement settled any disputes between the American settlers and the British, other disputes were still brewing in the Oregon territory. Indian frustrations were increasing; the Cayuse saw their land being taken piece by piece by the white settlers. The Indians also resented being told by missionaries that their cherished religious customs were sinful and would lead them to hell's fires. Moreover, the missionaries had brought with them an epidemic of measles. When the medical treatment given by the missionaries to the Indians failed and many Indian children died, the Indians held the settlers responsible. On November 29, 1847, Cayuse Indians launched a surprise attack on the mission founded by Marcus and Narcissa Whitman, killing the Whitmans and twelve others. In what became known as the Cayuse War, the settlers responded by burning Indian villages.

The Cayuse War was a tragic and bloody affair, but it had one positive result. The conflict forced Oregon settlers to seek a stronger government. In 1848, Congress officially established the Oregon Territory. Oregon City became the territory's first capital.

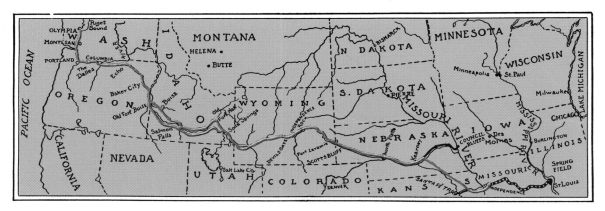

Ruts left by the wheels of wagon trains can still be seen along some sections of the Oregon Trail, which wound from Independence, Missouri, to the Oregon country.

THE OREGON TRAIL

"Wheat thrives astonishingly; I never saw better in any country, and the various vegetables are of the first quality." This account, written by a visiting scientist, was typical of those sent east by the first American settlers in Oregon. Such reports caused an outbreak of "Oregon fever" among townspeople in New England and farmers in the Midwest. The compelling Oregon fever caused easterners and midwestern farmers alike to pack their wagons and cross the continent.

Travelers on the Oregon Trail assembled in a jumping-off place such as Independence, Missouri. When spring grasses were sufficiently high to feed their cattle and oxen, they headed west, praying they would reach Oregon before winter snows closed the mountain passes. Their route followed three major rivers: the Platte over the Great Plains, the Snake in the Rocky Mountains, and finally the Columbia.

Each morning on the trail, the wagons pushed forward as cows mooed, dogs yelped, and wheels groaned. From the dusty grasslands of the Great Plains, the settlers struggled up the breathtaking Rocky Mountains. At the wilderness outpost of Fort Hall (in present-day Idaho), the westward trail branched. One branch led southwest toward California, while the other wound northwest to Oregon. Those who chose the path to Oregon crossed the Blue Mountains to arrive at the community of The Dalles on the banks of the Columbia River. Once there, the pioneers either boarded rafts and shipped their possessions to Oregon City, or struggled over a particularly difficult mountain pass through the Cascades. Ultimately, they arrived in the lush Willamette Valley.

The hazards men and women faced on the Oregon Trail were recorded in trail diaries. Some pioneers drowned during river crossings, while others toppled from cliffs or died trying to drive their wagons over mountains. The diary of one pioneer tells of this typical tragedy: "Mr. Harvey's little boy Richard, 8 years old, went to get on the wagon and fell. . . . The wheels ran over him and mashed his head."

Contrary to many movie westerns, Indian attacks on wagon trains were rare. Most Plains Indians who approached the travelers came to trade goods. However, gunfire flared when bands of whites or Indians tried to rustle the settlers' cattle. All things considered, cholera was the cruelest killer of travelers on the trail. By the time the Oregon Trail fell into disuse in the 1880s, nearly half a million men, women, and children had crossed it and at least thirty-four thousand of them died trying.

Despite the dangers, scarcity of food, and hardship, the trip had moments of warmth and joy. As Oregon Trail veteran Octavius Howe remembered:

Those who crossed the plains . . . never forgot the
ungratified thirst, the intense heat and bitter cold, the
craving hunger and utter physical exhaustion of the trail,
and the rude crosses which marked the last resting place of
loved companions. But there was another side. Neither
would they forget the level prairie, covered with lush
grass . . . the glorious sunrise in the mountains; the campfire
of buffalo chips at night. . . . True they had suffered, but the
satisfaction of deeds accomplished and difficulties overcome
more than compensated and made the overland passage a
thing never to be forgotten.

LIFE ON THE FRONTIER

The last page in the diary of one young frontiersman who
completed the journey over the Oregon Trail reads as follows:

Friday, October 27. Arrived at Oregon City on the falls
of the Willamette.
Saturday, October 28. Went to work.

The work of the Oregon pioneer was farming. Most farm
families cultivated wheat or oats. They quickly discovered that
corn could not withstand the cool nights of the Willamette Valley.

With no outside experts to give him advice, the pioneer farmer
had to be carpenter, veterinarian, and soil scientist. Frontier
fathers hunted and fished for recreation as well as to put food on
the family table. Women more often worked indoors or behind
the scenes, but pioneer Oregon depended on the frontier mother.
She cooked over a smoky fire, scrubbed clothes till her hands
blistered, and stayed up sewing by candlelight long after the rest
of the family went to bed. With few doctors available, it was up to
the pioneer mother to nurse a child through whooping cough or
measles. Children were expected to grow up fast and help out

In the 1850s, Oregon City was the largest town in the Willamette Valley.

with farm chores. Still, most went to school long enough to learn reading and simple arithmetic.

By 1850, small towns had sprung up in the Willamette Valley. Eugene, named after its first white settler, Eugene F. Skinner, began as a collection of farmhouses. Salem was a sleepy little hamlet until the territorial legislature moved the capital there in 1852. For a brief period in the 1850s, the legislature shifted the capital to the Willamette River port of Corvallis. Oregon City, which had served as the first territorial capital, was the region's largest town.

Located near the confluence of the Willamette and Columbia rivers, the town of Portland was a natural shipping center. It was also the farthest inland point on the Columbia River reachable by an oceangoing ship. For that reason, it overshadowed other river towns such as Milwaukie and Linn City. Soon the population of Portland surpassed that of Oregon City, and Portland became the largest town in the Pacific Northwest. Its two founders—both of whom were New Englanders—had disagreed over its name. Asa Lovejoy wanted to name the fledgling town "Boston," while Francis Pettygrove preferred "Portland" after his hometown in Maine. The two men flipped a coin, Pettygrove won, and today there is a Portland on both the Atlantic and Pacific coasts.

The discovery of gold in California in 1848 brought several changes to Oregon. An estimated two-thirds of the territory's men left their farms and headed to California dreaming of overnight wealth. Most, however, eventually returned. Those who had been successful brought desperately needed cash to the Oregon frontier. In addition, the increased demand furnished by California's growing population drove up prices for Oregon-raised wheat and other farm products.

The decade of the 1850s saw Oregon's white population explode from thirteen thousand to fifty-two thousand. Two major factors spurred this spectacular growth. First, in 1850, Congress passed the Oregon Donation Land Law. The law offered a man and his wife up to 640 acres (259 hectares) of land in Oregon Territory if they agreed to cultivate it for four years. The Donation Land Law was one of the most generous land-giveaway programs in American history. Soon after, in 1851, gold was discovered along Jackson Creek in southern Oregon, and the territory experienced a gold rush of its own.

BOOM TIMES

In southwestern Oregon, boomtowns sprouted up almost overnight. Jacksonville instantly became the largest city between San Francisco and Portland. Jacksonville was not a pretty sight. The city was a haphazard collection of tents and log cabins, and its main street was lined with saloons and gambling houses. Other boomtowns in the south included Kerby, Phoenix, Galice, and Gold Hill. Along the southern coast, gold was found at Pistol River, Port Orford, and Gold Beach.

The mining boom brought work-hungry Chinese immigrants to the territory. Whites began to resent the Chinese laborers, who were willing to work for low wages. Under pressure from whites, the Oregon territorial legislature passed a law forbidding Chinese from owning mining operations. The territory's gold rush began a long period of Asian discrimination in Oregon.

In southwest Oregon, the by-products of mining fouled the streams fished by Indians. Miners killed the animals the Indians depended on for food and often drove the Indians from their lands. These abuses touched off the Rogue River War, which raged on and off between the Indians of southwest Oregon and territorial militia between 1851 and 1856.

In 1861, the precious yellow metal was discovered a few miles south of the John Day River, and the lure of gold brought people to undeveloped eastern Oregon. As had been true in the southwest, boomtowns—such as Canyon City and John Day—suddenly popped up. For a brief period, the eastern mining town of Auburn had a population of six thousand and was Oregon's largest city. Then the gold ran out, and today Auburn does not even appear on the map.

Oregon's gold rush helped the territory's economy in many ways. Portland and The Dalles, both of which were key supply points for the eastern gold fields, enjoyed dizzying growth. Steamboat travel on the Columbia flourished. Ranchers discovered that the eastern grasslands were excellent grazing lands for cattle. Cattle towns such as Prineville, Lakeview, Burns, and Pendleton soon developed.

Cattle towns such as Pendleton developed after the discovery of gold brought
settlers to eastern Oregon in the early 1860s.

STATEHOOD

The Oregon Territory that had been established in 1848 was
huge. As more settlers streamed in, the United States Congress
divided the Oregon Territory into several smaller territories. In
1853, Congress established Washington Territory to the north,
thereby determining Oregon's current northern border.
Washington Territory was later extended to the southeast, giving
Oregon its present eastern border.

In 1857, Oregon voters approved a plan that would allow
Oregon Territory to become a state. At the time, the United States
Congress was deadlocked over the issues of slavery and states'
rights, and the Oregon application was delayed. Finally, on
February 14, 1859, Oregon was admitted as the nation's thirty-
third state. The state constitution rejected slavery but excluded
free blacks from the state. However, the latter condition was
seldom enforced. Salem was named the state capital, and John
Whiteaker became the state's first governor.

Shortly after Oregon achieved statehood, the nation was torn
apart by the bloody Civil War. Many Oregonians were pro-Union

Chief Joseph

A Nez Percé holding a traditional war pole

and antislavery, but they were far from the fighting fronts and had little influence on the war's conduct. The war did have an influence on Oregon, however. Oregonians were now forced to defend their frontiers from Indian attacks without the help of federal troops. Indian wars in the eastern and southern parts of the state raged on and off through most of the 1860s and into the 1870s.

In 1872-73, an outbreak of bitter violence known as the Modoc War occurred. The Modocs were protesting their confinement on a reservation already occupied by the Klamaths. Fifty Modoc warriors held back a thousand United States troops in the desolate landscape of the Lava Beds near the Oregon-California border. The hostilities ended when the Modoc leader known as Captain Jack was captured and hanged for killing General E.R.S. Canby and a Methodist minister.

THE NEZ PERCÉ SAGA

Like many other tribes of the Northwest, the Nez Percé people had occupied their homeland for many generations. Part of the tribe's domain, the beautiful Wallowa Valley of northeast Oregon, included some of the finest grazing land anywhere in the United States. In the 1800s, this land was coveted first by gold seekers and then by powerful cattle barons. The federal government tried to buy the land from the Nez Percé, but their leaders, led by Old Chief Joseph, refused to sign the treaty. Regardless of this, years later the federal government ordered this group of Nez Percé to move to a reservation in Idaho. To government officials, Young Chief Joseph, the son of the old chief, quoted the last words of his dying father: "My son. . . . This country holds your father's body. Never sell the bones of your father and mother." When Chief Joseph's people refused to move, war broke out.

Chief Joseph was an orator and a religious leader, not an experienced warrior. Yet he, along with the war chiefs Looking Glass and White Bird, led his people on a brilliant march that kept United States troops at bay for nearly four months. As the Nez Percé traveled toward safety in Canada, newspapers chronicled how Nez Percé men, armed with primitive rifles, outfoxed and outfought the well-equipped cavalry troops who pursued them. But the Nez Percé were woefully outnumbered and had scant supplies. American troops finally surrounded the Indians when they reached the Bear Paw Mountains in Montana, just a day's ride from Canada. After a five-day battle in the mountains, the Nez Percé were forced to surrender.

The Nez Percé conflict of 1877 was the last major Indian war fought in the Pacific Northwest. Upon surrendering, Chief Joseph conceded the end of Indian power in the region by giving one of the most moving speeches in American history: "It is cold and we have no blankets. The little children are freezing to death. . . . Hear me, my chiefs! I am tired. My heart is sick and sad. From where the sun now stands I will fight no more forever."

Chapter 6
OREGON LEADS THE WAY

OREGON LEADS THE WAY

As the twentieth century began, Oregon was a leader among the states in enacting political and social reforms. For this reason, Oregon soon gained a reputation as one of the nation's most progressive states.

RAILROADS AND THE GROWTH OF INDUSTRY

In 1883, the industrial age was welcomed to Oregon by a brassy and joyous parade through the streets of Portland. At the front of the parade were fifty weathered men, all of whom had crossed the continent by way of the Oregon Trail. Behind the men rumbled a hissing and spitting steam locomotive. It was the very first train to reach Oregon over the Northern Pacific line, which connected the Pacific Northwest with the eastern half of the country. Now goods shipped in and out of Portland could easily be transported to and from the state's interior—as well as to areas east of Oregon.

Local railroads had operated in Oregon since the 1860s. The state's most ambitious effort in railroad construction in the late 1860s was a line through the Willamette Valley connecting Portland and San Francisco. That project, financed by businessmen Ben Holladay and Henry Villard, took twenty years to complete. Soon railroads snaked beyond the Cascade Mountains and into Oregon's interior. Houses, farms, and businesses clustered everywhere the railroads went. The iron giants brought in hordes of new Oregonians.

Aided by the railroads, armies of loggers cut into the thick stand of trees that guarded the Columbia River from the Pacific coast to the Hood River. The forests were so rich and dense that one acre (two-fifths of a hectare) of those lush Columbia forests yielded more logs than five acres (two hectares) of timberland in other parts of the country. With the advent of the railroads, the lumber industry was no longer dependent on rivers and waterways for transportation. The railroads were extended to the Blue Mountains, where there were more seemingly limitless forests. The logging companies were eager to reach Oregon's forests. The pinelands of Michigan and Minnesota had already been thinned, but the national demand for wood products still remained high.

Railroads helped develop Oregon's interior as businesses exploited the "3 Gs": gold, grass, and grain. Gold mining was augmented by the extraction of silver, lead, and mercury from the eastern hills. The flat land and bunchgrass of central and southern Oregon east of the Cascades were exploited for cattle ranching. Sheep raising was introduced on the grasslands of north-central Oregon, and the tiny railroad stop of Shaniko became one of the world's largest wool centers. Checkerboard patterns of wheatfields appeared in the northeast as farmers discovered that wheat thrived in the river valleys.

New industrial workers, many of them foreign-born, flocked to Oregon. Finns came to Astoria, where they found work in the city's fish-canning factories. Basques from northern Spain came to tend sheep in the central grasslands. Chinese continued to journey to Oregon to work in the mines. Japanese labored on railroad construction and in lumber mills. Soldiers from both sides of the Civil War came to Oregon after the hostilities ended. The population of Oregon exploded from fifty-two thousand in 1860 to nearly three hundred thousand in 1890.

Oregon's industrial growth in the late 1800s brought immigrants of many ethnic groups to the state, including Chinese (top left), Basques (top right), Finns (bottom left), and Japanese (bottom right.)

This 1873 cartoon depicts the Grange, represented by a farmer, attempting to alert the country to the abuses of the railroad industry.

But the economic growth triggered by the railroads came at a high price. While aiding industrial expansion, railroad owners also gouged farmers and workers and bought the votes of state politicians.

THE PROGRESSIVE YEARS

In the 1870s, Oregon was a land in revolt. Farmers decried the high freight rates charged by railroads to ship farm products to market. Industrial workers demanded minimum-wage laws and compensation for injuries suffered on the job. Small businesses sought the regulation of banks. When these citizens took their demands to Salem, however, they discovered that the legislature was dominated by unresponsive corporate giants.

Gradually, progressive and reform-minded Oregonians organized to regain control of their government. In 1873, various farmers' organizations banded together to found the Oregon State Grange. The Grange was an offshoot of a national organization that pressured state governments to regulate the railroad industry. In 1892, the People's (or Populist) party, also backed by the farmers, began to gain strength in Oregon. Its leader, Sylvester Pennoyer, had become governor of Oregon as a Democrat in 1887. Governor Pennoyer advertised himself as a man of the people, but he often played on the fears of whites. Pennoyer claimed that the continuous stream of Chinese immigrants would erode the Oregon way of life. Although the Populist party kept the flame of reform alive, it was unable to pass many progressive laws.

THE OREGON SYSTEM

Progressive-minded Oregonians sought a new leader who could bring intelligence and energy to their cause. In 1889, William U'Ren, a Wisconsin-born lawyer, journeyed to Oregon. Soon, he became the heart and soul of the state's reform movement. U'Ren was not a professional politician—he served only one term in the Oregon legislature. Instead, he worked behind the scenes of government, forming organizations such as the District Legislation League and the People's Power League. These groups advocated changes to the lawmaking process that would allow voters to create laws directly by initiative rather than only by relying on appeals to their state legislators.

U'Ren and the other supporters of Oregon's Progressive movement won heartening victories in Oregon. In 1902, the state adopted initiative and referendum procedures. These procedures allow ordinary citizens to make new laws or rescind old ones. In 1908, Oregonians enacted a recall law that gave voters the power to remove state officials whom the voters deemed undesirable. The new, more direct influence of the voters resulted in a number of reforms, including the creation of a state commission to regulate banking and control the freight rates charged by railroads. Workers won a minimum-wage law, and voters passed an ordinance prohibiting child labor in Oregon.

Three major factors contributed to the Progressives' success in Oregon. First, the Progressives were able to form a coalition of farmers, workers, and owners of small businesses. Second, the Progressive movement was blessed with remarkable political leadership. In addition to U'Ren, Senator Jonathan Bourne and Portland Mayor (and later U.S. Senator) Harry Lane were dynamic Progressive leaders. Third, in Oregon the reformers found involved voters who were willing to read the lengthy and often densely written laws that they were called upon to approve or turn down. This novel form of government could succeed only with the help of active and literate citizens.

In the early 1900s, a wave of progressive political thinking swept the United States, and its supporters pointed proudly to the Oregon success story. Reformers hailed Oregon as the "most complete democracy in the world." Soon, the adoption of direct legislation became known as the "Oregon System."

A landmark Progressive victory came in 1912, when women in Oregon won the right to vote. Abigail Scott Duniway led the state's woman suffrage fight. At seventeen, she had crossed the Oregon Trail, losing both her mother and a brother during the journey. After marrying a farmer, she helped to support her family by running a women's hat shop in Albany. In 1871, she, her husband, and their six children moved to Portland. There, the entire Duniway family worked to publish a weekly newspaper called the *New Northwest*. The paper printed local news and became a powerful voice of the women's rights movement. Using the initiative and referendum laws to their advantage, women's rights groups put a suffrage amendment on the ballot. After being

Abigail Scott Duniway, shown here registering to vote for the first time, led the battle for woman suffrage in Oregon in the early 1900s.

defeated three times, the proposal was finally passed, and Oregon became one of the first states to extend voting rights to women.

OREGON IN A CHANGING WORLD

In the early 1920s, some of Oregon's citizens became intrigued—briefly—with the Ku Klux Klan. The Klan was anti-black, anti-Catholic, and anti-Jewish; it seemed to be the antithesis of Oregon's Progressive tradition. The white-supremacist group made inroads in many states after World War I. In Oregon, the Klan backed a proposal to close all of Oregon's private schools, many of which were operated by the Catholic church. The proposal was passed by an initiative in 1922, but was declared unconstitutional by the Supreme Court in 1925. After several years, the Klan's influence diminished in the state.

One of Oregon's most important political figures in the first half of the twentieth century was Charles L. McNary, a Republican who served in the United States Senate from 1917 until his death in 1944. McNary, from an old pioneer family, was trusted by farmers and workers. In 1924, as an early champion of conservation, McNary sponsored a law to provide more land for national forests and to promote government-lumber industry cooperation in reforestation. McNary was the vice-presidential running mate of Republican Wendell Wilkie in 1940, but that ticket lost by a large margin to President Franklin D. Roosevelt.

The Great Depression of the 1930s devastated Oregon's economy. Factories closed and farmers and ranchers went bankrupt. The federal government offered relief in the form of the Bonneville Dam project. This project poured $70 million into building the massive Bonneville Dam on the Columbia River. Located about forty miles (sixty-four kilometers) east of Portland, the dam took seven years to complete, and thousands were employed during its construction. When finished, the dam provided low-cost electricity and made the Columbia navigable as far as The Dalles.

World War II made new demands on the state's farms and factories. Portland's port facilities shipped supplies to the Russian allies as well as to United States armed forces in the Pacific. Aluminum plants opened in the city of Troutdale, where the Bonneville Dam supplied plenty of inexpensive electricity. Industrialist Henry Kaiser built many of his cargo-hauling "Liberty" ships and other types of ships in Portland. By manufacturing huge sections of the ships separately and then assembling the sections in the Portland shipyards, Kaiser was able to churn out new ships at an astonishing speed. One World War II Liberty ship was assembled in a record ten days.

World War II brought the state a great domestic tragedy. After Pearl Harbor was attacked by the Japanese, Americans of Japanese

After Japan bombed Pearl Harbor, Portland shipyards produced hundreds of ships for the war effort (left). Japanese Americans who lived near the coast were forced to evacuate their homes and move to "relocation centers" such as this one at Heart Mountain, Wyoming (above).

ancestry, even those born in America, were suspected of being spies. These suspicions persisted even though no shred of evidence existed to support any claims of disloyalty. As a result, the government forced all persons of Japanese heritage who lived in western California, Oregon, and Washington to leave their homes and move to barbed-wire-enclosed compounds for the remainder of the war.

The postwar years were a period of adjustment for Oregon. Wartime industry had brought 160,000 new workers to the state. Many of the new Oregonians were black or Hispanic. Portland's black population zoomed from two thousand in 1940 to twenty thousand in 1945. Thousands of Hispanics came to Oregon through the federally sponsored *Bracero* program, which encouraged farm workers to leave Mexico and become field hands in the United States.

THE ENVIRONMENT AND THE ECONOMY

The Willamette River had once been a place where people swam and fished. The water was clean enough to drink. By the end of World War II, however, industrial pollution and sewage from cities had killed off the fish, and no one swam in the river any longer. A government report written in the 1950s said, "From Eugene to its confluence with the Columbia, the Willamette [is] the filthiest waterway in the Northwest and is one of the most polluted in the nation."

In 1961, a local television station produced a documentary exposing industrial pollution of the Willamette. The program was so shocking that many industrial plants threatened to sue. The producer of the documentary was newsman Tom McCall. In 1966, McCall ran for governor of Oregon. His victory was based largely on his promise to clean up the state's environment. The river was cleaned up at the expense of the industrial plants, and the dumping of pollutants ceased. For the first time in decades, salmon returned to the Willamette. A strict law governing water-quality standards was then extended to every river and stream in the state. The state legislature also passed a controversial law that required city and county land-use planning. Oregon even enacted a unique "bottle bill," which required all drinks to be sold in returnable cans or bottles in order to discourage people from littering. The 1960s also brought the beginning of a crusade to limit private development along the Oregon coast. By the early 1970s, Oregon's environmental-protection laws were hailed by many conservationists as the nation's finest.

As Oregon entered the 1970s, its service industries, such as wholesale and retail trade, developed. Once again, thousands of new migrants from California and other industrialized states streamed to Oregon. Some Oregonians worried that their state would become overcrowded and urged the government to discourage this influx. Echoing this sentiment, Governor McCall told a convention of out-of-staters, "Welcome to Oregon. While you're here I want you to enjoy yourselves. Travel, visit, drink in the great beauty of our state. But for God's sake, don't move here."

This sentiment changed in the 1980s as a stagnant state economy became Oregon's most important concern. Fewer Americans built new homes during the early 1980s, and the lumber industry began to slump. Oregon's unemployment figures skyrocketed, becoming among the highest in the nation.

To help new industries become established, many state politicians discussed changing the state's "antibusiness" image. Any person or company who would pump money into the sluggish economy was urged to move to Oregon. Governor Victor Atiyeh sounded the call for change by declaring, "Oregon is open for business."

In the late 1980s, the economy continued to be helped by the growth of the high-technology industry, which had begun in the 1940s. American and Japanese firms built electronics and computer plants in various parts of the state. Oregon is blessed with an educated and energetic work force, making the state a natural target for high-tech industries. Also, the state's dazzling natural scenery has continued to attract tourists. As newly elected Governor Neil Goldschmidt said in 1987, "Oregon is a state rich in natural beauty, in the strength of its citizens and its institutions."

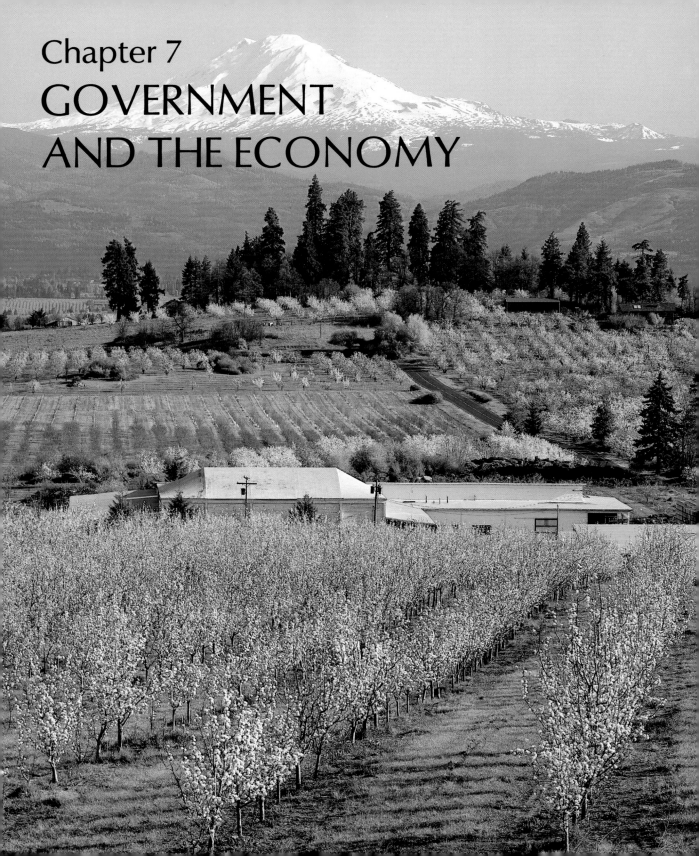

Chapter 7

GOVERNMENT AND THE ECONOMY

GOVERNMENT AND THE ECONOMY

GOVERNMENT

Oregon is governed by a constitution that was written in 1857, two years before Oregon became a state. The constitution may be amended by a majority vote of the legislature and by the approval of the voters in the next regular general election. True to the tradition of initiative and referendum, the voters may amend the constitution directly as well. A petition signed by 8 percent of the voters will put a proposed amendment on the ballot during a regularly scheduled election, and if a majority of the electorate approves, the amendment will be added to the constitution.

The Oregon constitution divides the state government into three branches: the executive, which carries out laws; the legislative, which creates laws; and the judicial, which interprets the law and tries cases.

The executive branch is headed by the governor, who is elected to a four-year term. Oregon is one of the few states that has no lieutenant governor. The governor has broad powers, including the right to appoint heads of departments and to call out the state militia in times of emergency. Other executive officers (all of whom are elected for four-year terms) include the attorney general, secretary of state, superintendent of public education, and treasurer.

The state capitol in Salem

The legislative branch, called the Legislative Assembly, is made up of a thirty-member senate and a sixty-member house of representatives. Senators are elected to four-year terms; members of the house serve two-year terms. State legislators debate proposed laws, called bills. When a majority agrees on the details of a bill, it is sent to the governor. The governor may sign the bill into law, or refuse to sign (veto) it. A vetoed bill may be returned to the legislature. If both houses approve it by a two-thirds majority, the bill becomes law regardless of the governor's wishes.

Writing a budget is usually the most fiercely debated activity of state government. The average yearly expenditure of the Oregon state government amounts to more than $12 billion. The state receives funds from a personal income tax, from the federal government, from taxes on certain items such as liquor and gasoline, and, since 1985, from a state lottery.

The highest court in Oregon's judicial branch is the state supreme court. The Oregon Supreme Court has seven justices, all of whom are elected to six-year terms. The Oregon Court of Appeals is the next-highest court. The state has a system of circuit courts made up of eighty-four judges divided among nineteen districts. The court system hears cases ranging from serious crimes to squabbles between neighbors.

Local government in Oregon is divided into 36 counties and more than 240 incorporated towns and cities. The state constitution gives counties and towns broad home-rule powers, meaning that towns have the right to choose their own form of government. Providing a police force and street and park maintenance are some of the services furnished by local governments.

EDUCATION

Funding the vast public-school system is the most expensive function of state government. Total school expenditures reach about $1.5 billion each year.

State law requires Oregon children to attend school from the ages of seven to seventeen. The Oregon public-school system supports vocational schools, a school for the blind, and a school for the deaf. Although private and parochial school attendance is growing in Oregon, the overwhelming majority of students go to public schools.

Higher education in Oregon centers around eight public four-year colleges and universities and twenty private colleges. The largest institution of higher learning is the state-supported University of Oregon at Eugene. Other large state-supported schools include Portland State University, Oregon State University

in Corvallis, and Southern Oregon State College in Ashland.
Major private colleges include Lewis and Clark College in
Portland, Linfield College in McMinnville, Pacific University in
Forest Grove, Reed College in Portland, and the University of
Portland. Willamette University in Salem, founded in 1842, is the
oldest university west of the Mississippi River.

AGRICULTURE

The *Oregon Bluebook*, published by the state government, claims,
"Oregon agriculture is perhaps the most diverse of any
comparable geographic area on earth. No fewer than 172 [crops]
are produced within the state."

Oregon's many different land regions allow the state to produce
an incredible variety of crops. Cranberries grow well along the
coast. Hay, fruit, nuts, vegetables, and a host of other crops are
grown in the fertile Willamette Valley. The plateau region of
north-central Oregon is perfect for growing wheat. Sheep graze on

Oregon's many different land regions allow the state to produce a wide variety of crops. Traveling across the state, one might encounter everything from fields of baled hay (left on opposite page), to a tulip farm (above), to grazing land for cattle or sheep (top right), to a mist-shrouded pear orchard (bottom right).

grasslands in southwestern Oregon, in the Willamette Valley, and on the eastern ranges. Beef cattle are raised on the eastern ranges as well. Juicy apples and pears are grown in the Mount Hood region. The region around The Dalles is cherry country. Sugar beets come from the Snake River region. Potatoes are grown in the rich soil along the Deschutes and John Day rivers and in the far eastern part of the state. Dairy cattle and flower bulbs are cultivated in western Oregon. Nearly all the nation's hazelnuts, as

Oregon is the nation's leading producer of timber.

well as seeds for ornamental grasses, come from Oregon. The state
is also a leading producer of peppermint oil.

Oregon has about thirty-seven thousand farms. Although only
4 percent of Oregonians work in agriculture, the state's farms
produce $2 billion a year in farm products. In terms of cash sales,
cattle ranks first, wheat second, and hay third. The state's average
farm covers 486 acres (197 hectares). However, a vegetable farm
in the Willamette Valley may be only one-tenth that size, while a
wheat farm in the northeast will spread over ten times the average
area. About 99 percent of Oregon's farms are owned by families
who view farming as a way of life as well as a business.

MANUFACTURING

Some two hundred thousand workers, 20 percent of the state's
labor force, hold manufacturing jobs. Oregon's factories produce
$8 billion worth of goods each year.

The logging industry provides thousands of jobs in Oregon. After the trees are cut down, the logs are loaded onto trucks (left). Some are transported to sawmills, where they are cut into lumber (above).

Wood products are the state's leading manufactured items. Oregon sawmills produce lumber for construction businesses around the country. The state's paper mills turn out millions of tons of paper and paper products every year. Oregon is one of the country's leading suppliers of plywood. Eugene is a major center for lumbering and the manufacture of wood products.

The exciting field of high technology is Oregon's fastest-growing industry. In the mid-1980s, Oregon was home to nearly four hundred high-tech firms that employed 33,620 workers and had a total payroll of $1 billion. In the early 1990s, high-tech employment is expected to double. High-tech companies in Oregon produce computer components, electrical equipment, and precision instruments.

The state's food-processing industry enjoys more than $1 billion in annual sales. Working closely with farmers, food-processing firms freeze, can, and freeze-dry foods to prepare them for store

71

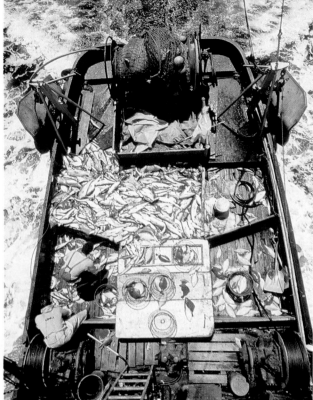

Commercial fishermen in Oregon haul in
many kinds of fish, including red
snapper (above) and bottom fish (right).

shelves. Factories in Tillamook County process raw milk into
cheese. Fruits and vegetables are canned in many of the state's
cities. Nyssa is home to processing plants that make sugar from
sugar beets.

NATURAL RESOURCES

Oregon mines turn out $130 million in raw materials each year.
The mines yield industrial materials such as gypsum as well as
metallic ores such as gold, silver, iron, copper, and bauxite. The
state also has vast deposits of limestone, sand and gravel, and
pumice; and small amounts of nickel and subbituminous coal.

Commercial fishing, one of Oregon's earliest industries, remains
a thriving enterprise. Commercial fishermen haul in about 100
million pounds (45 million kilograms) of fish each year. Salmon is

the state's most valuable catch, followed by tuna, flounder, oysters, rockfish, and white sturgeon.

Vast forests remain the state's richest natural resource. Oregon has led the nation in timber production every year since 1938. Providing 76,000 direct jobs, the forest-products industry is by far the state's biggest employer. Estimates indicate that an additional 150,000 people are employed indirectly by furnishing goods and services to the lumber businesses.

Oregon exports many of its forest products. The Port of Coos Bay is one of the largest shippers of forest products in the world. However, the extensive export of raw logs has caused some uneasiness. The Oregon exports keep many foreign sawmills busy while mills in Oregon stand silent.

In recent years, the state has carefully controlled lumbering. Logging companies are required to plant trees to replenish the forests. Furthermore, the state government has stipulated that some 2.1 million acres (.85 million hectares) of valuable forestland be withheld from lumbering. Conservationists especially object when lumber companies cut into "old-growth" forests (forests that are more than two hundred years old). The conflict between the needs of conservation and economic growth is continual in Oregon.

SERVICE INDUSTRIES

Service industries account for nearly 70 percent of the state's gross product. Wholesale and retail trade is the state's most important service industry. Portland, the commercial center of the state, leads the Pacific Northwest in wholesale trade. The port cities of Astoria and Coos Bay are also centers of international trade. East of the Cascades, The Dalles, Pendleton, Bend, and

A crowd gathers to watch a newly restored Southern Pacific Railroad train
leave Portland's Union Station for the first time.

Klamath Falls are retail and service centers for their regions.
Businesses relating to tourism are the third-largest employer in
the state. The millions of tourists who flock to Oregon spend
about $2.6 billion a year for tourism-related services.

TRANSPORTATION AND COMMUNICATION

Oregon's network of roads totals 141,096 miles (227,066
kilometers). Interstate 5, which crosses the width of the state from
the California border through the Willamette Valley to Portland,
can be thought of as the state's "lifeline" because it connects many
of Oregon's major cities.

Railroads run on about 3,000 miles (4,828 kilometers) of track.
Although passenger service is declining, the trains still haul

Portland is the West Coast's third-busiest port.

thousands of tons of freight. Oregon has 423 airports. Portland
International Airport is the state's largest airport.

Even though Portland lies about 100 miles (161 kilometers)
from the Pacific Ocean, it is the state's major seaport. In total
commerce, Portland is the West Coast's third-busiest port, trailing
only the California cities of Long Beach and Los Angeles. The
Columbia River near Portland is a virtual superhighway of huge
ships. The Dalles and Umatilla are other Columbia River ports.

About 125 newspapers, including 21 dailies, are published in
Oregon. The largest circulation is enjoyed by the *Oregonian* of
Portland, followed by the *Eugene Register-Guard* and the *Statesman-
Journal* of Salem. Oregon has about 140 radio stations and 16
television stations.

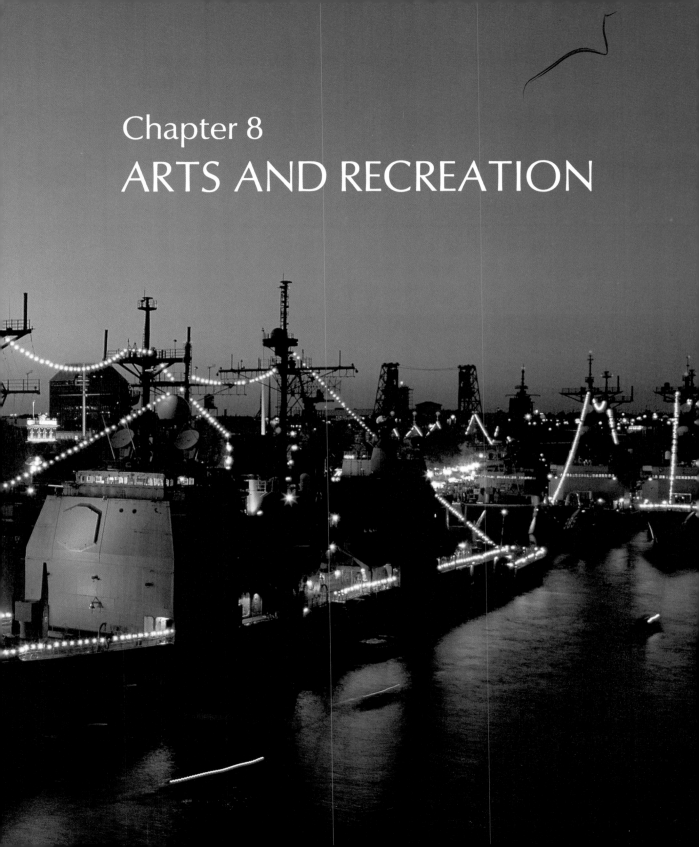

Chapter 8
ARTS AND RECREATION

ARTS AND RECREATION

THE FINE ARTS

Native American basket weavers were among Oregon's first artists. Using multicolored grasses, ancient craftsmen wove brilliant geometric images into their baskets.

Artists came to Oregon to record the expeditions of the earliest white explorers. Englishman Henry Warre rendered oil paintings of Fort Vancouver and Oregon City in the 1840s. Warre's paintings are now studied by historians. In the 1850s, John Mix Stanley painted portraits of famous Oregon pioneers, including John McLoughlin, the Father of Oregon.

Near the turn of the century, Portland became a haven for sculptors. In 1888, the city's Skidmore Fountain was unveiled. Stephen Skidmore, who wanted to give Portland a monument dedicated to "horses, men, and dogs," commissioned artist Olin Warner to design the fountain. In 1905, Portland sculptor Alice Cooper unveiled her statue *Sacajawea*, a life-size bronze monument of the Shoshone woman who participated in the Lewis and Clark Expedition to the Pacific Ocean.

In the 1930s and 1940s, the Portland Art Association sponsored an art school whose leading teachers were painters Harry Wentz and Clayton "C.S." Price. Wentz, who was born in The Dalles, painted marvelous watercolors of Oregon's rugged mountains and seacoast. Price was a largely self-taught "cowboy artist" who was

The Skidmore Fountain
by Olin Warner is
a Portland landmark.

born in Montana. Wentz, Price, and the art association's dedicated curator, Anna Belle Crocker, helped Portland become an exciting art center.

Oregon painters Carl Morris, Louis Bunce, and Michele Russo flowered in the 1950s. These three painters of nature scenes found inspiration in Oregon's outdoor wonders. After the 1950s, Oregon artists experimented with abstract forms. Many Oregon artists of the time were influenced by painters from Asia. Modern paintings and sculpture are displayed at the Portland Center for The Visual Arts. Opened in 1972, the center is one of Portland's most popular gathering places for artists.

Pietro Belluschi and John Yeon were two of Oregon's leading architects. Champions of an architectural movement known as the

Timberline Lodge was built in the 1930s as a WPA project.

Northwest Style, they favored buildings designed to flow naturally into their environment. Italian-born Belluschi described one of his houses as "clean and simple but not modernistic — above all . . . in harmony with the hills and Oregon firs." Belluschi achieved fame in the 1930s when he designed the Portland Art Museum in Portland. John Yeon designed residential homes for Portland families. One of the state's most noteworthy architectural landmarks is Timberline Lodge on Mount Hood. Designed by architects associated with the WPA projects of the 1930s, the lodge is made entirely from local materials and contains many fine wall murals and wood sculptures.

LITERATURE

Indian storytellers once told of a legendary time when Oregon was young, and magic and mystery shrouded the land. In those days, there was a natural bridge across the Columbia River at what is now the town of Cascade Locks. To guard the bridge, the Great Spirit chose a lovely Indian squaw named Loo-Wit. His sons, Klickitat and Wyeast, both fell in love with Loo-Wit and began fighting over her. They growled, stamped their feet, blew smoke and fire, and then hurled hot rocks at each other. Finally they threw so many rocks on the bridge that it collapsed. The Great Spirit was so angry that he turned them into mountains— Loo-Wit became Mount St. Helens, ever young and beautiful; Klickitat became Mount Adams; and Wyeast is now Mount Hood.

Such Indian folktales were the beginnings of Oregon literature. The tales were memorized by storytellers and passed orally from one generation to the next.

Written descriptions of Oregon began with the arrival of the fur traders and the explorers. One chronicle, written in 1778, was Jonathan Carver's *Travels Through the Interior Parts of North America*. This book contains the first written reference to the "River Oregon [the Columbia] or River of the West that flows into the Pacific . . ." Several years later, William Cullen Bryant romanticized the river and the region with a poem that included these lines:

Or lose thyself in the continuous woods
Where rolls the Oregon, and hears no sound
Save its own dashings.

Many historical novels, factual accounts, and trail diaries describe experiences on the Oregon Trail. Oregon pioneers wrote about their struggles on the frontier in such books as T.T. Geer's *Fifty Years in Oregon* and Thomas Nelson Strong's *Cathlamet on the Columbia*.

Two of Oregon's most talented writers emerged at the end of the nineteenth century. In 1890, Oregonian Frederic Homer Balch

John Reed (left) and Ken Kesey (above) are two of Oregon's noted literary figures.

published his mystical novel *The Bridge of the Gods.* Set in an Oregon of fabled times, it told of the destruction of the legendary natural bridge that once crossed the Columbia. Journalist John Reed, born to a wealthy Portland family in 1887, traveled to Russia as a young man. Reed wrote a powerful account of the 1917 Russian Revolution in his book *Ten Days That Shook the World.* A dedicated Communist, Reed was buried in front of the Kremlin (the headquarters of the Soviet government), and he is now hailed as a hero in the Soviet Union.

Many Oregon writers of the 1930s and 1940s looked back to their state's pioneer era as a setting for stories. H.L. Davis's 1935 novel *Honey in the Horn* received the Pulitzer Prize in 1936 and became a bestseller. The novel told of homesteaders trying to farm the inhospitable high-desert lands of eastern Oregon. Mary Jane Carr, who specialized in writing young people's books, set her popular novel *Children of the Covered Wagons* on Oregon's frontier.

Ken Kesey is one of Oregon's most famous modern writers.

Oregon's majestic mountains and sparkling rivers and lakes invite windsurfers (top left), kayakers (bottom left), and skiers (above).

Kesey grew up in Springfield and graduated from the University of Oregon at Eugene in 1957. Both of his two best-selling novels had Oregon settings. *One Flew Over the Cuckoo's Nest* is the story of a young man judged insane and confined to a mental hospital. *Sometimes a Great Notion* tells of the conflicts between two brothers against the background of the rough-and-tumble logging business.

Ursula Le Guin, a longtime resident of Portland, is an acclaimed author of science-fantasy novels and children's books.

SPORTS

Oregon's diverse land regions allow a person to ski in the Cascades in the morning and then drive to the coast for late-afternoon skin diving. Forests and streams invite canoeing,

Eugene, known as the "Track and Field Capital of the World," hosts many important track events.

fishing, hiking, and camping. Team sports are played in all school gymnasiums and public parks.

The University of Oregon campus at Eugene is a legend in the world of track and field. Eugene's year-round mild weather provides a superb training ground for runners. In fact, the city has been dubbed the "Track and Field Capital of the World." Eugene hosts such important track meets as the USA/Mobile Championships and the U.S. Olympic Track and Field Trials. Such Olympic stars as Mary Decker Slaney, Steve Prefontaine, and Alberto Salazar have lived and trained in Eugene.

The Portland Trail Blazers of the National Basketball Association are the state's major professional sports team. Since the team's creation in 1970, the Trail Blazers have seen years of glory and years of bitter disappointment. Oregon sports fans still

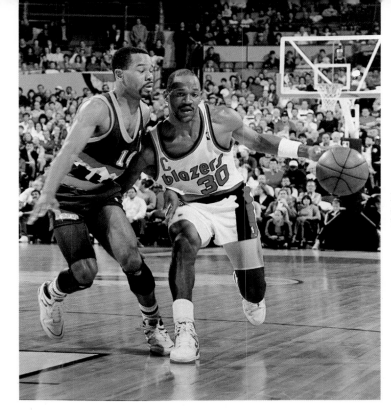

Portland is the home of the NBA Portland Trail Blazers.

talk about the 1977-78 season, when the "Blazers" powered their way to an NBA championship. The team was led by Bill Walton, the dominating center from UCLA. Assisting Walton were a squad of unselfish players that included power forward Maurice Lucas and guards Lionel Hollins and Dave Twardzik. "They played team ball," said the team's owner, Larry Weinberg, after the Blazers won the crown. "They are the embodiment of what is best in pro basketball."

FAIRS AND FUN

In the 1800s, cowboys and loggers enjoyed gathering together to display their skills. Oregonians keep this tradition alive in rodeos and lumber contests. The World Championship Timber Carnival is held in Albany every Fourth of July weekend. Contestants compete in events such as ax throwing, tree chopping, and

A hot-air balloon race is one of the events of the annual Portland Rose Festival.

logrolling. The work of the cowboy, so often celebrated in American movies, is honored every September during Pendleton's Round-Up Week. The town of St. Paul also holds a rodeo, and the All-Indian Rodeo is staged in the Tygh Valley in mid-May.

Music and theater are celebrated at many Oregon festivals. The Oregon Shakespearean Festival, held each summer in Ashland, is world famous. In 1983, the festival won the coveted Tony Award for outstanding achievement in regional theater. Its productions feature costumes and stage decorations that replicate those used during Shakespeare's time. The music of Johann Sebastian Bach

The All-Indian Rodeo is held every year in the Tygh Valley.

fills the air during the Bach Summer Music Festival in Eugene. The Peter Britt Music and Arts Festival, held every August in Jacksonville, brings together professional musicians whose styles range from classical to bluegrass. As many as twenty thousand people attend the annual Mount Hood Festival of Jazz.

"To every thing there is a season, and a time to every purpose under heaven," says a Psalm in the Bible. Oregonians honor the gifts of the seasons with city and county fairs. Perhaps the most famous of these fairs is the seventeen-day-long Portland Rose Festival, held in June, when the roses are in their full glory. The fair is highlighted by parades and sporting events, all staged amidst Portland's riot of roses. The strawberry-producing city of Lebanon, in the Willamette Valley, holds its Strawberry Festival in early June. Every year, city leaders create the "world's largest strawberry shortcake" as a centerpiece for the fair.

Chapter 9
A TOUR OF OREGON

A TOUR OF OREGON

American writer Pearl S. Buck once said, "It takes centuries for
a people to realize and sufficiently love the beauty of places such
as Oregon." Certainly no vacationing family will have centuries to
see the wonders of the Beaver State, but even a quick zigzag
through the state can fill a traveler with enough memories to last
a lifetime.

THE EAST

Along the Idaho border in northeast Oregon is Hells Canyon, a
fantastic gorge carved thousands of years ago by the restless Snake
River. In some places, Hells Canyon drops a dizzying 8,000 feet
(2,438 meters), making it the deepest canyon in North America.
Several footpaths wind down the canyon walls, but potential
hikers should be in superb physical condition to attempt them.
The climb in and out of Hells Canyon is a marvelous but
exhausting experience.

The peaks of the Wallowa Mountains are so magnificent that
residents of Wallowa County call their region the "Switzerland of
America." The Blue Mountains, which begin near the city of La
Grande, offer what many winter-sports enthusiasts claim are
Oregon's finest ski slopes.

The city of Pendleton serves as headquarters for northeast
Oregon's cattle, sheep, and wheat industries. Famed for its Round-
Up rodeo, Pendleton advertises itself as "not the New West, not
the Old West, but the REAL West."

90

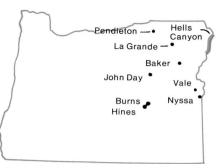

The Snake River flows through Hells Canyon, the deepest canyon in North America.

Thick forests, majestic mountains, and sprawling rangeland cover much of northeast Oregon. Umatilla National Forest is famed for its vast marshlands, which serve as the winter home of some ninety thousand Canada geese and two hundred thousand ducks.

To the south are towns whose historical roots date to the state's gold-rush and cattle-kingdom eras. Baker, a gold-rush town, boasts a marvelous collection of nineteenth-century buildings, many of which have been carefully restored to look as they did in their glory days. The city of John Day is a market center for cattle ranchers, and cowhands on horseback still drive livestock through its streets. The fossilized remains of plants and animals that lived in eastern Oregon as early as 30 million years ago have been uncovered at John Day Fossil Beds National Monument, made up of three separate areas east of John Day.

Southeast Oregon is a land for people who enjoy wide-open spaces. The southeast is made up of three gigantic counties—Lake, Harney, and Malheur—which cover 28,450 square miles (73,686

Cathedral Rock at John Day Fossil Beds National Monument

square kilometers) but contain only 42,850 people. This sheep and cattle region is crowded with natural wonders, however. For instance, the Hart Mountain National Antelope Range near Lakeview includes almost 250,000 acres (almost 101,000 hectares) of land covered with sagebrush and juniper trees and populated by pronghorn antelope, bighorn sheep, and mule deer. Fremont National Forest, west of Lakeview, beckons hikers with wilderness trails.

Along the Idaho border, the city of Nyssa stands in the heart of a rich agricultural region known as the Treasure Valley. The nearby city of Vale was once a stopping point on the Oregon Trail. Farther west, Burns and its neighbor Hines are business centers for the region's farmers and ranchers. Hines originated as a lumber-mill town. North of these two cities are Malheur and Ochoco national forests, which shelter a fantastic variety of wildlife.

Cascade Locks
Columbia River Gorge
Troutdale
The Dalles
Hood River
Madras
Deschutes River
Prineville
Redmond
Bend

A wild-horse drive near Bend

CENTRAL AND NORTH-CENTRAL OREGON

The central Oregon towns of Prineville, Madras, and Redmond serve as starting points for the adventurous breed of treasure hunters who call themselves rockhounds. In the nearby hills, the rockhounds search for thunder eggs (the state rock), agates, and other semiprecious stones.

During presidential elections, political pollsters from as far away as Japan and Switzerland come to Prineville to ask the citizens which candidate they will vote for. Prineville is the seat of Crook County, the only county in the nation that has voted for every presidential candidate to win the popular vote since Grover Cleveland in 1884.

Once an Indian trail juncture, the city of Bend is today a crossroads community where several highways converge. The largest city in central Oregon, Bend is blessed with a breathtaking Cascade Mountains backdrop. A short drive from Bend is the High Desert Museum, where plant and animal life typical of the high desert is displayed. The Deschutes River, which begins in the Cascade Mountains southwest of Bend and flows north to the

The Columbia Gorge Hotel in Hood River

Columbia River, is recognized as one of Oregon's finest white-water attractions.

A few miles west of where the Deschutes River flows into the Columbia is the city of The Dalles. Once the last stop on the Oregon Trail, The Dalles is now a river port and a thriving farming center. The town holds a Cherry Festival every April.

Farther west along the Columbia, resting in the shadows of the Cascades, is the city of Hood River. Hood River's popular Port Marina Park offers fishing, swimming, board-sailing, and boating on the sparkling Columbia.

The Columbia River Gorge is one of Oregon's—and the nation's—most famous scenic marvels. The portion of the gorge between The Dalles and Troutdale, with its waterfall-draped basalt cliffs, has been designated a National Scenic Area.

Near the city of Cascade Locks, a steel bridge crosses the Columbia at the same spot where, legends claim, an angry god

Visitors to the Bonneville Dam (left) can watch salmon travel up man-made fish ladders (above).

once destroyed a natural bridge. This modern bridge is called, appropriately, The Bridge of the Gods.

West of Cascade Locks along the Columbia River is the Bonneville Dam. The dam's fish ladders—long sets of watery steps built to give the river's salmon a passageway upstream—become a scene of high drama during the spawning season. Obeying their instincts to travel upstream, the salmon struggle up this man-made ladder to lay their eggs in the quieter waters beyond the dam. The salmons' graceful leaps in the air are a sight guaranteed to be etched in a visitor's memory forever.

THE WILLAMETTE VALLEY

Farmers have a saying to describe especially rich soil: "Plant a broomstick and it will grow." No doubt, that old expression has been used many times in connection with the Willamette Valley. More than a century ago, the fertile valley was the magnet that drew thousands of families over the Oregon Trail.

The area around Cottage Grove is famous for its covered bridges.

At the southern end of the Willamette Valley is the town of Cottage Grove, renowned for its rustic covered bridges. Farther north along Route 5 is Eugene, Oregon's second-largest city. Eugene is a city of athletes, boasting running trails and bicycle paths that wind along the banks of the Willamette River. A favorite hiking path starts south of downtown and winds 3.5 miles (5.6 kilometers) up the 2,000-foot (610-meter) mountain called Spencer Butte. Art lovers flock to Eugene's many galleries and to the University of Oregon's Museum of Art, famed for its Oriental collection.

To the north, Brownsville, Sweet Home, and Lebanon are market communities for nearby farms, as well as stopovers for tourists heading toward the Cascade Mountains. Corvallis (whose name evolved from a Latin phrase meaning "the heart of the valley") is a lovely college town that served for a short time as Oregon's territorial capital. The Horner Museum in Corvallis has an excellent display of pioneer and Indian artifacts. The city of Albany was founded in 1848 by Walter and Thomas Monteith, who named the settlement after their hometown in New York.

Many of Albany's houses, built more than a century ago, are architectural gems. Dallas and Independence are other mid-valley towns with proud pioneer histories. Philomath has a small museum where visitors can study the region's past.

Salem, the state capital, lies in the heart of the Willamette Valley. The state capitol building houses a superb display on Oregon history. Across the street spreads the campus of Willamette University, the oldest college in the western United States. A short walk takes a visitor to Mission Mill Village, a complex of historical buildings that includes a nineteenth-century woolen mill.

The town of Woodburn is home to large Spanish-speaking and Russian-speaking communities. In the spring the town celebrates Cinco de Mayo, a Mexican festival; and Russian Easter, an important Russian Orthodox holiday. Nearby Aurora is famed for its antique shops. McMinnville is a wine center with a number of excellent restaurants. Graceful old houses are a feature of Newberg. The Minthorn house in Newberg was the boyhood home of Herbert Hoover, the thirty-first president of the United States. As a teenager, the future president spent one summer earning fifty cents a day picking onions on a Newberg farm.

THE PORTLAND AREA

Few cities are as blessed by nature as is Portland. The Willamette River flows through its heart. The mountains of the Coast Range rise to the west, while snowcapped Mount Hood— the king of the Cascades—towers over the city to the east. Portland has more than 160 parks, and it seems as if a new fountain appears at every street corner. Its climate, despite winter fog and drizzles, is pleasant, and flowers bloom year-round. It is

The Portland riverfront at dusk

no wonder that Portland has been called America's most livable large city.

Pioneer Courthouse Square serves as Portland's main plaza. The square opened in 1983 after forty-eight thousand citizens helped finance its construction by buying personalized bricks. On nearby Park Avenue stands the Portland Art Museum, known for its outstanding collection of Northwest Coast Indian art; and the Oregon Historical Society Museum, which chronicles the state's past. Old Town is a rehabilitated wharf section that was once the hangout of hard-drinking sailors, dock workers, and loggers. Portland's Governor Tom McCall Waterfront Park is a lovely lane

Portland's many beautiful gardens include the Japanese Garden (left) and the Crystal Springs Rhododendron Garden (above).

of grass and flowers that stretches twenty blocks along the riverfront.

Washington Park, in the West Hills, is a favorite recreation area for Portlanders. A highlight of the park is the Japanese Garden, five acres (two hectares) of delicate flowers, shrubs, and cherry trees. A breathtaking view of the area is offered at the Pittock Mansion, an elegant French Renaissance-style structure. Just down the hill, Portland's world-famous Rose Test Garden blossoms with ten thousand rosebushes of four hundred varieties.

The Washington Park Zoo houses a wide variety of animals, including a prized collection of Asian elephants. The World Forestry Center presents information on forest-resource management and the wood-products industry. The nearby Oregon Museum of Science and Industry includes fascinating electronics displays and a planetarium.

North of Washington Park is Forest Park, 5,000 acres (2,023 hectares) of magnificent woodland with 30 miles (48 kilometers) of hiking trails. Forest Park is probably the only place in the United States where a person can become lost in the woods without stepping beyond the city limits.

Portland offers a wealth of cultural activities. The Oregon Symphony performs at the downtown Schnitzer Concert Hall. Chamber Music Northwest gives its concerts at Catlin Gable School and at Reed College. Free "brown-bag" concerts are given at various places in the city to entertain people on their lunch breaks. Jazz lovers rave about the city's wide variety of jazz clubs. Young writers read poems and short stories at the coffee shop attached to gigantic Powell's Bookstore. Portland theaters offer everything from Broadway musicals to experimental plays. Visitors who get hungry while seeing the sights can stop at one of Portland's twelve hundred restaurants. Chinese, Vietnamese, and Japanese restaurants are especially popular in the city.

Many interesting communities lie a short ride away from downtown Portland. The city of Beaverton is noted for its high-tech firms. Forest Grove holds a vintage car show each July. Oregon town history began at Oregon City, founded in 1842 by John McLoughlin. McLoughlin's restored home is one of Oregon City's most popular tourist attractions.

THE OREGON COAST

The Oregon coast is lined with more than fifty state parks — where the view belongs to everyone. The coast has many small communities, but only two towns with populations of more than ten thousand. The coast is a playground for sea lions, waterfowl, and occasional schools of humpback whales. It is nature's art gallery, displaying mighty cliffs sculptured by centuries of wind and surf.

Astoria
Cannon Beach
Tillamook
Newport
Florence
Winchester Bay
North Bend
Coos Bay
Charleston
Port Orford
Gold Beach
Brookings

Wind-sculpted trees dot the landscape at Ecola State Park on the north coast.

The city of Astoria is the largest community on the north coast. Astoria was the first permanent white settlement in Oregon. Nearby, at Fort Clatsop National Memorial, is a replica of Fort Clatsop, where Lewis and Clark wintered in 1805. Astoria is also the home of the Columbia River Maritime Museum, which has an outstanding display of ship models.

Fort Stevens State Park stretches between Warrenton and Hammond along the north coast. The park has miles of bicycle paths and hiking trails along the beach. The coastal city of Seaside holds a rugged twenty-six-mile (forty-two-kilometer) Trail's End Marathon race every February. The residents of nearby Cannon Beach sponsor a gentler competition—the annual Cannon Beach Sand Castle Contest.

Cheesemaking is the major industry in the north coast town of Tillamook. Residents there have a saying that Tillamook is a "town of trees, cheese, and ocean breeze." At Cape Meares stands

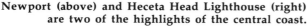
Newport (above) and Heceta Head Lighthouse (right) are two of the highlights of the central coast.

a restored lighthouse, one of a string of weathered old lighthouses that rise like sentinels guarding the Oregon coast. Near the lighthouse is the often-photographed Octopus Tree, an oddly formed spruce that looks like a huge octopus stuck in the sand.

U.S. Highway 101, a two-lane road, is Oregon's major coastal highway. Oregon writer Paul Lucas described Highway 101 in these words: "The coast highway bravely follows the contours of this wild and intricate shoreline, sometimes lifting high up and over the Pacific on a sheer cliff face, then zooming down and around a little bay almost at eye level. In the tortured dance it must do to get through this obstacle course, it is a wriggling snake. . . ."

Newport, on Oregon's central coast, is a sport-fishing center. Each morning, boats carrying eager fishing enthusiasts churn out to the deep seas. Legend has it that the nearby Yaquina Bay Lighthouse is haunted by the ghost of a girl who disappeared mysteriously while visiting the structure a century ago.

Left: Oregon Dunes
National Recreation Area
Above: Sea Lion Caves

Sea Lion Caves, near the city of Florence, is one of the coast's most enduring attractions. An elevator that plunges 2,000 feet (610 meters) takes visitors down to a broad, balconylike cliff. Below spreads a secluded beach where a hundred or more sea lions frolic. The adult sea lions waddle about the rocks barking furiously, while the cubs splash in the waves. The nearby Heceta Head Lighthouse is one of Oregon's most famous coastal shrines.

South of Florence spreads Oregon Dunes National Recreation Area. Visitors explore the area's lovely white sand dunes on foot, in dune buggies, and even on camelback. Nearby Winchester Bay is home port for Oregon's largest fleet of sport-fishing boats. Anglers also praise the fishing near the tiny town of Lakeside.

The south coast begins at Coos Bay. The Coos Bay Area includes the picturesque waterfront towns of North Bend, Coos Bay, and Charleston. With twenty-five thousand people living in the area, Coos Bay has the greatest population of the otherwise uncrowded south coast.

Visitors can watch enormous waves crash into the cliffsides at Shore Acres State Park.

Sunset Bay State Park has a picturesque natural bay enclosed by towering sandstone cliffs. Just to the south is Shore Acres State Park, where visitors can watch for whales from a glass-enclosed shelter overlooking the ocean and jagged cliffs. When the sea is raging at Shore Acres, enormous whitecapped waves thunder into the cliffsides, sending clouds of spray 50 feet (15 meters) into the air. Such a spectacle breeds a special kind of coastal visitor called a "wave watcher."

At Port Orford, Humbug Mountain—the second-highest peak on the Oregon coast—rises 1,756 feet (535 meters) above the Pacific. Inland from Port Orford lies a colossal meteor that crashed into the land in the early 1860s. The meteor weighs as much as a World War II tank.

The 36-mile (58-kilometer) journey from Gold Beach to Brookings takes the visitor along the most spectacular stretch of

Sunrise at Siskiyou National Forest in southwestern Oregon

the Oregon coast. The fabulous ocean scenery here includes fantastic rock formations, the highest bridge in Oregon, and a view of a forest plunging down to the sea. Loeb State Park gives visitors a double treat. On the east end of the park are cliffs and pounding surf, while just 1 mile (1.6 kilometers) inland rises a magnificent stand of redwood trees.

SOUTHWESTERN OREGON

Southwestern Oregon is dominated by the Klamath Mountains, which sweep from the coast to the Cascades. Mountain scenery and lively towns make the southwest one of the state's most interesting areas.

The Siskiyou National Forest has Douglas fir trees that are more than eight centuries old. The forest also has twenty-seven other

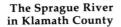
The Sprague River
in Klamath County

types of evergreens. Its variety of trees makes Siskiyou one of the
most diverse forests in the world. Oregon Caves National
Monument, farther east, is a fascinating labyrinth of limestone
caves.

Interstate 5, the state's "lifeline," enters Oregon from California
and winds through the region's major towns. Ashland, home of
the renowned Oregon Shakespearean Festival, is southern
Oregon's cultural capital. The city of Medford, which serves a rich
fruit-growing region, holds a Pear Blossom Festival every April.
History comes alive in Jacksonville, which has carefully preserved
many of the houses built during the mining boom of the 1850s.
The entire town, in fact, has been designated a National Historic
District. Grants Pass is located along the Rogue River, a favorite
waterway for devotees of canoeing, kayaking, and rafting.

Klamath Falls, which boasts about 290 days a year of sunshine,
rises in the center of more than one hundred lakes and streams in
Klamath County.

Many tourists claim that Crater Lake is the most unforgettable
sight in the Beaver State. Formed some seven thousand years ago

Crater Lake, one of the world's scenic wonders, is the deepest lake in the United States.

when an eruption blew the top off ancient Mount Mazama, Crater Lake lies silent, still, and almost mystically blue. Two islands in the middle of the lake seem to float on its surface like timeless ships. The lake is surrounded by Crater Lake National Park, which contains nearly 200,000 acres (81,000 hectares) of forests interlaced with hiking trails.

Crater Lake—a natural wonderland—is a fitting place to end a tour of Oregon. As one Beaver State historian has noted, "Oregon's relationship to nature is more noticeable than in most of the fifty states." The state's most stunning natural gift is its uncommon beauty. Veteran travelers often argue the question: which is the most attractive state in the land? Many travelers cast their vote for Oregon.

STATE OF OREGON

1859

FACTS AT A GLANCE

GENERAL INFORMATION

Statehood: February 14, 1859, thirty-third state

Origin of Name: The word *Oregon* (sometimes spelled *Origan* or *Ouragon*) was an early name for the river now called the Columbia. Eventually, the region drained by the river became known as the Oregon country, and finally, the state took the name.

State Capital: Salem

State Nickname: ''Beaver State''

State Flag: The two-sided, navy-blue flag of Oregon was adopted in 1925. On one side is a gold beaver. On the other side is a gold replica of the state seal, surrounded by thirty-three stars.

State Motto: She Flies With Her Own Wings

State Bird: Western meadowlark

State Animal: Beaver

State Insect: Oregon swallowtail butterfly

State Fish: Chinook salmon

State Flower: Oregon grape

State Tree: Douglas fir

State Rock: Thunder egg (geode)

State Gemstone: Sunstone

State Dance: Square Dance

State Song: "Oregon, My Oregon," words by J.A. Buchanan, music by Henry B. Murtagh; adopted in 1927:

Land of the Empire Builders,
Land of the Golden West;
Conquered and held by free-men,
Fairest and the best.
Onward and upward ever,
Forward and on, and on;
Hail to thee Land of heroes,
My Oregon.

Land of the rose and sunshine,
Land of the summer's breeze;
Laden with health and vigor,
Fresh from the Western seas.
Blest by the blood of martyrs,
Land of the setting sun;
Hail to thee Land of Promise,
My Oregon.

POPULATION

Population: 2,633,149, thirtieth among the states (1980 census)

Population Density: 28 people per sq. mi. (11 people per km²) (1988 estimate)

Population Distribution: About 61 percent of Oregon's people live in cities or towns. Nearly 43 percent of the state's population live in the Portland metropolitan area.

Portland	366,383
Eugene	105,624
Salem	89,233
Springfield	41,621
Corvallis	40,960
Medford	39,603
Gresham	33,005
Beaverton	30,582
Hillsboro	27,664

(Population figures according to 1980 census)

Population Growth: Oregon's population nearly doubled every ten years from the opening of the Oregon Trail in the 1840s until the end of the nineteenth century. The population surged again in the mid-1900s. In the 1940s, jobs in wartime industries drew people to the state. In the 1970s, jobs in the service industries brought people to Oregon. The state's population grew by 26 percent from 1970 to 1980, while the population of the entire country grew by only 11.45 percent. The list below shows population growth in Oregon since 1860:

Year	Population
1860	52,465
1880	174,768
1900	413,536
1920	783,389
1940	1,089,684
1960	1,768,687
1970	2,091,533
1980	2,633,149

GEOGRAPHY

Borders: Oregon is bordered by Washington on the north, Idaho on the east, and Nevada and California on the south. The Pacific Ocean determines Oregon's western border.

Highest Point: Mount Hood, 11,239 ft. (3,426 m)

Lowest Point: Sea level, along the Pacific Ocean

Greatest Distances: East to west—401 mi. (645 km)
North to south—294 mi. (473 km)

Coastline: 295 mi. (475 km) (about 400 mi. [644 km] including bays and peninsulas)

Area: 97,073 sq. mi. (251,419 km²)

Rank in Area Among the States: Tenth

Indian Reservations: The 1980 census estimated Oregon's Native American population at 27,309. Most Indians in Oregon are associated with one of eight federally recognized tribes within the state. About 25 percent of the people live on one of Oregon's reservations: Warm Springs, Umatilla, Burns Paiute, and Siletz. Together these reservations total 814,434 acres (329,593 hectares), about 1 percent of the state's land area.

Rivers: Oregon's two major rivers are the Columbia in the north and the Snake in the east. The Columbia River is the nation's third-longest river, with a total length of about 1,215 mi. (1,955 km). It forms most of the border with Washington and allows the inland city of Portland to serve as an ocean port. The Columbia's major tributary is the 250-mi. (402-km) Willamette River. Other important tributaries are the Deschutes, John Day, and Umatilla rivers; and Rock and Willow

Rabbitbrush along Crump Lake in the south-central part of the state

creeks. Together, these waterways drain nearly 60 percent of the state. The Snake River makes up the northern half of Oregon's border with Idaho. Major tributaries of the Snake River include the Imnaha, Powder, Burnt, Malheur, and Owyhee rivers. Other large rivers in Oregon include the Rogue River, the Sprague River, and Silver Creek. Hundreds of rapids and waterfalls are formed as swiftly moving streams plunge down Oregon's mountain slopes. Among the best-known falls are Bridal Veil, Horsetail, Latourell, Multnomah, and the group of eleven falls in Silver Creek Falls State Park.

Lakes: Oregon's more than six thousand lakes range from small ponds to artificially created lakes and dams that cover more than 1,000 acres (405 hectares). Crater Lake, in the Cascade Mountains, is the nation's deepest lake, at 1,932 ft. (589 m). Roughly circular in shape, it lies in the crater of an extinct volcano. Other major lakes in the Cascades include Waldo and Diamond lakes and Howard Prairie Reservoir. Oregon's largest natural lake is Upper Klamath Lake in the south-central part of the state. Although quite shallow, it spreads over 143 sq. mi. (370 km ^{2}). Harney and Malheur lakes are important lakes located in the southeast region of the state.

Topography: The lofty Cascade Mountains run from north to south through Oregon and divide the state into two distinct regions. Between the Pacific Ocean and the Cascades is a green, lush region of abundant rainfall; east of the Cascades, the land is much drier and the vegetation is sparser.

The unusual growth of these mountain hemlocks in Mount Hood National Forest was probably caused by a long-ago rock slide.

About one-third of the state lies west of the Cascades. This area includes the Coast Range, a narrow strip of mountains that extends northward from the Coquille River. The Coast Range stands parallel to much of Oregon's Pacific coastline. At the coastline, sheer cliffs, some as high as 1,000 ft. (305 m), rise from a coastal plain that is never more than a few miles wide. Rolling and forested, the Coast Range is cut by numerous streams and small valleys. To the south are the rugged Klamath Mountains. The state's richest mineral deposits are found in the thick forests of these mountains. To the north, sandwiched between the Coast Range and the Cascades, is the Willamette River Valley. The fertile soil and mild climate of the Willamette Valley has made it Oregon's richest farming and industrial area.

The Cascade Mountains contain Oregon's highest peaks, including Mount Hood and Mount Jefferson. The rugged western slope of the Cascades rises steeply from the Willamette Valley floor. The gentler eastern slope merges into a high, semi-arid plateau.

A region known as the Columbia Plateau stretches eastward from the Cascades to the Blue and Wallowa mountains in northeastern Oregon. This plateau, or tableland, is often rugged and rocky and is deeply cut by river canyons. Much of the land is used for raising cattle or growing wheat. The Blue and Wallowa mountains offer spectacular gorges, scenic mountain lakes, extensive forests, and rich deposits of minerals.

The Basin and Range Region of southeastern Oregon is a semi-arid land characterized by ridges and buttes alternating with basins containing shallow lakes.

A winter scene along Warm Springs River on the Warm Springs Indian Reservation

Climate: Oregon's climate is affected by the Cascade Mountains. West of the Cascades, the climate is tempered by mild, moist winds that sweep in from the Pacific Ocean. The weather is mild and humid, with moderate temperatures and abundant rainfall. Along the coast, temperatures average 45° F. (7° C) in January and 60° F. (15.5° C) in July. Average annual precipitation (rain and snow) on the coast is 80 in. (203 cm), although parts of the Coast Range average 130 in. (330 cm) a year. The Willamette Valley, east of the Coast Range, shares the pleasant weather of the coast, with slightly higher temperatures and annual average precipitation of 40 in. (102 cm). Winter fog is common in the valley; in Portland, the sun shines only about 48 percent of the time on winter days.

Blocked off from the mild, moist Pacific air by the Cascades, eastern Oregon is colder in winter, warmer in summer, and generally drier than the western third of the state. Temperatures average 27° F. (-3° C) in January and 72° F. (22° C) in July, with a year-round threat of sudden and extreme temperature changes. Oregon's highest and lowest temperatures were both recorded in this area. In 1898, a high of 119° F. (48° C) was set at Prineville on July 29 and at Pendleton on August 10. In 1933, a low of -54° F. (-48° C) was set at Ukiah on February 9 and at Seneca on February 10. Annual precipitation in eastern Oregon averages 6-12 in. (15-30 cm), with relatively high precipitation falling (as snowfall) in the Blue and Wallowa mountains.

Portland's Washington Park Rose Garden

NATURE

Trees: Oregon has nearly eighty native species of trees. The most common trees are alders, ashes, cedars, cottonwoods, firs, hemlocks, junipers, madrones, maples, oaks, pines, spruces, and willows.

Wild Plants: Included among Oregon's more than two thousand species of wild plants are azaleas, buttercups, currants, Indian pipes, laurels, lupins, trilliums, violets, manzanita, bitterbrush, Scotch broom, Oregon grape, sagebrush, and salmonberry.

Animals: Antelopes, beavers, bighorn sheep, black bears, bobcats, coyotes, deer, elk, foxes, mountain goats, mountain lions, minks, muskrats, nutrias, opossums, river and sea otters, rabbits, sea lions, seals, squirrels, lizards, salamanders, snakes

Birds: Oregon is home to more than a hundred species of songbirds. Larger birds include chuckar partridges, cormorants, cranes, ducks, falcons, geese, grouse, gulls, owls, pelicans, pheasant, plovers, quail, snipe, swans, and turkeys. The state is on the Pacific Flyway, a major migratory route for birds.

Fish: Bass, cod, halibut, herring, perch, sablefish, salmon, sole, sturgeon, tuna, steelhead, brook, and rainbow trout

GOVERNMENT

The government of Oregon, like that of the federal government, is divided into three branches: executive, legislative, and judicial.

Oregon's legislative branch, called the Legislative Assembly, consists of a thirty-member upper house, called the senate, and a sixty-member lower house, called the house of representatives. State senators are elected to four-year terms. State representatives are elected to two-year terms. During legislative sessions, which begin on the second Monday of odd-numbered years, the legislators vote on new laws and determine how state revenue will be spent.

The judicial branch consists of a supreme court, a court of appeals, and lower courts. The Oregon Supreme Court has seven justices who are elected to six-year terms. The justices of the supreme court elect one of their number to be chief justice for a six-year term. The court of appeals has ten judges who are elected to six-year terms. Circuit-court judges are elected for six-year terms by a nonpartisan ballot from each of the state's nineteen judicial districts. Other lower courts include district, county, justice, and municipal courts. Oregon has had a special tax court since 1961.

The governor executes, or carries out, the law. The governor of Oregon is elected to a four-year term, and cannot serve more than eight years during any twelve-year period. The governor appoints the heads of many state departments, has the power to veto legislation, and is the commander-in-chief of the state militia. Oregon has no lieutenant governor. Other elected officials include the secretary of state, attorney general, superintendent of public education, and state treasurer.

Number of Counties: 36

U.S. Representatives: 5

Electoral Votes: 7

EDUCATION

Oregon state law requires that all children between the ages of seven and seventeen attend school. Oregon has 305 locally elected school boards that operate 1,233 elementary and secondary schools. Oregon also has approximately 500 private elementary and secondary schools. The Oregon public-school system supports vocational education, a school for the blind, and a school for the deaf.

Oregon has eight public four-year colleges and universities, fifteen public community colleges, and twenty private four-year colleges. The University of Oregon at Eugene, with more than seventeen thousand students, is the state's largest university. Other large state-supported universities include Oregon State University at Corvallis and Portland State University. Private colleges and universities of note include the University of Portland, Linfield College in McMinnville, Lewis and Clark College in Portland, Pacific University in Forest Grove, and Reed College in Portland. Willamette University in Salem, founded in 1842, is the oldest college west of the Mississippi River.

**Benton Hall
at Oregon State
University in
Corvallis**

ECONOMY AND INDUSTRY

Principal Products:
Agriculture: Beef cattle, dairy cattle, wheat, barley, oats, hay, rye, grass seed, greenhouse and nursery products, hops, flower bulbs, hazelnuts, berries, cherries, plums, pears, apples, cranberries, peppermint, green peas, onions, potatoes, snap beans, sugar beets, sweet corn, chickens, hogs, sheep
Manufacturing: Lumber and wood products, food products, scientific instruments, nonelectrical machinery, aircraft equipment, computers and computer software, paper products, electrical machinery and equipment, fabricated metal products, furniture, primary metals, printing and publishing, transportation equipment
Natural Resources: Forests, water, fertile soil, nickel, limestone, sand and gravel, clay, copper, diatomite, fish, gemstones, gold, gypsum, lead, mercury, natural gas, coal, pumice, silver, talc

Business and Trade: Twenty percent of the state's work force is employed in manufacturing. Wood products are the state's most-important manufactured items. Oregon, which supplies nearly 20 percent of the nation's lumber, leads the nation in the production of lumber and plywood. About 76,000 people are directly employed in the forest-products industry, and another 150,000 of the state's jobs are dependent on lumbering. Food processing, which generates more than $1 billion per year in sales, is the second-most-important manufacturing endeavor. The paper-products industry and high-tech industries also make significant contributions to the state's economy.

Service industries account for more than two-thirds of the gross state product. Wholesale and retail trade provide 19 percent of the state's gross product and employ nearly one out of every four Oregonians. Tourism, finance, insurance, and real estate are other important service industries in Oregon.

Coos Bay ships more forest products than any other port in the world.

Communication: Oregon has about 125 newspapers, of which 21 are dailies. Established in 1850 as the *Weekly Oregonian*, the *Oregonian* is the state's oldest and largest-circulating paper. Other important newspapers include the *Eugene Register-Guard*, Medford's *Mail-Tribune*, Salem's *Statesman-Journal*, and Albany's *Democrat-Herald*. Oregon has about 140 radio stations and 16 commercial television stations. There are also 32 public radio and television stations in the state. More than 160 Oregon communities are served by cable television.

Transportation: Oregon has 141,096 mi. (227,066 km) of roads and highways. Interstate Highway 5 is an important north-south route across the state. Interstate Highway 84 runs east-west from Ontario to Portland. Major railroads operating in Oregon include the Southern Pacific, Union Pacific, and Burlington Northern. Portland International Airport is the largest of the state's more than four hundred airports. It is served by thirteen major commercial airlines, as well as two regional and seventeen all-cargo airlines. Eugene, Medford, and Klamath Falls are also served by major commercial airlines.

Although situated about 100 mi. (161 km) inland, Portland is a major seaport. It is, after Long Beach and Los Angeles, the third busiest on the Pacific coast. Coos Bay ships more forest products than any other port in the world. Twenty-one other Oregon cities are either coastal or river ports.

The Portland Center for the Performing Arts

SOCIAL AND CULTURAL LIFE

Museums: The Portland Art Museum houses one of the Pacific Northwest's largest collections of Northwest Indian, Asian, and European art. The Portland Center for the Visual Arts specializes in contemporary paintings, sculpture, video-art shows, and the performing arts. The Oregon Historical Center in Portland has a large collection of Indian and pioneer artifacts and more than 1.5 million historical photos. Portland's Children's Museum is scaled for children and has many touchable items. The Portland Museum of Science and Industry in Washington Park attracts both children and adults with its many hands-on exhibits and its Kendall Planetarium. Specialized museums in Portland include the Advertising Museum; the Oregon Maritime Center and Museum; and the Portland Police Historical Museum, which includes exhibits of police badges, uniforms, and other police memorabilia.

The Museum of Art at the University of Oregon in Eugene is famed for its Oriental collection. The Desert Museum near Bend features live exhibits of the desert's ecosystem. The Flavell Museum in Klamath Falls and the Horner Museum in Corvallis both have many exhibits of Indian artifacts. The Kam Wah Chung Museum in John Day is a restoration of a trading post that served Chinese miners during the 1860s. The Jacksonville Museum in Jacksonville is widely acclaimed for its excellent exhibits of early Oregon life; a children's museum is housed next door in an old jail.

Libraries: Oregon has 204 public libraries, 125 specialized libraries, and 44 academic libraries. The Multnomah County Public Library in Portland, with more than 1.3 million volumes, is the state's oldest and largest public library. Large academic libraries are located at the University of Oregon at Eugene and Oregon State University at Corvallis. The Oregon State Library, in Salem, has nearly

119

1.4 million cataloged items, including more than 860,000 government documents
and 135,000 microforms. The state also has many specialized libraries.

Performing Arts: The Oregon Symphony, founded in 1896, performs more than
a hundred concerts a year. Based in Portland, where it performs at the Arlene
Schnitzer Concert Hall, the orchestra also performs in many other Oregon and
Washington cities. The Portland Opera Association stages four major productions
each year at the Schnitzer Concert Hall. The Portland Youth Philharmonic is a
training orchestra for players under the age of twenty-one. Since 1980, the West
Coast Chamber Orchestra has given a series of concerts at Portland State
University's Lincoln Hall. Free chamber-music concerts are performed each year
by the Portland Chamber Orchestra at the Portland Art Museum. A chamber-music
series is held each year at Portland State's Lincoln Hall under the sponsorship of
the Friends of Chamber Music. Every summer, Reed College sponsors a music
series known as Chamber Music Northwest. The internationally acclaimed Oregon
Bach Festival and the Eugene Festival of Musical Theater are held every summer in
Eugene. Jazz lovers flock to the University of Portland's Festival of Jazz in March,
and the Mt. Hood Festival of Jazz in August.

Among Portland's many dance groups, the best known is Ballet Oregon, which
presents everything from ballet to jazz. Other performing groups include the
Pacific Ballet Theatre, Osland and Company/Dance, Judy Patton Company, Oregon
Dance Consort, the Dancers Workshop, and the Echo Theatre/Do Jump Movement
Theatre. The Eugene Ballet has received national recognition.

The Oregon Shakespearean Festival (O.S.F.), in Ashland, attracts audiences from
all over the United States for its renowned performances of Shakespeare's comedies
and tragedies. The O.S.F. expanded recently, opening the Portland Center Stage at
the Intermediate Theatre of the brand-new Portland Center for the Performing
Arts. The New Rose Theatre, the Portland Civic Theatre, and the Portland
Repertory are among Portland's resident companies.

Sports and Recreation: Oregon's only major professional sports team is the
Portland Trail Blazers of the National Basketball Association. The Portland Beavers
are the AAA farm team of the Minnesota Twins baseball team. The Portland Winter
Hawks compete in the Western Hockey League. For many years, Oregon State
University has been a basketball powerhouse; many of its stars have gone on to
play in the NBA. Every winter, the Portland Memorial Coliseum is host to the Far
West Classic basketball tournament.

Camping along Scout Lake in the Mount Jefferson Wilderness

A number of top regional and national track meets are held in Eugene, long the training ground of many famous track-and-field stars. The Portland Invitational Indoor Track and Field Meet is held on the last Saturday in January. Long-distance running is a popular sport in Oregon. Major long-distance races include the Steve Prefontaine 10K run in Coos Bay and the Trail's End Marathon in Seaside.

With its diverse climate, 340 state parks and recreation areas, 14 national forests, and Wild and Scenic River System, Oregon has something for everyone who enjoys the outdoors. Oregon also has a national park, Crater Lake National Park; and national monuments at Oregon Caves and the John Day Fossil Beds. Boating and fishing enthusiasts enjoy Oregon's 6,000 lakes, more than 50,000 mi. (80,465 km) of rivers and streams, and 400-mi. (644-km) coastline. Oregon's rivers offer everything from floating, fishing, and drifting to exciting white-water rafting. More than 120 golf courses dot the Oregon landscape. Rockhounding is popular in all parts of the state. In the winter, Oregon offers skiing, skating, snowmobiling, and cross-country skiing. Fourteen locations have chair-lift service for downhill skiing.

Historic Sites and Landmarks:

Astoria is the site of Oregon's first permanent settlement, founded as a trading post by John Jacob Astor's Pacific Fur Company in 1811.

First Christian Church in Pleasant Hill, organized in 1850, was the first of its denomination in Oregon. Nearby Pleasant Hill Cemetery is one of Oregon's oldest settler burial grounds.

The Pittock Mansion in Portland

Fort Clatsop National Memorial, near Astoria, is a reconstruction of the fort where Lewis and Clark wintered in 1805-06. The museum in the visitor's center has many exhibits relating to the famous transcontinental expedition.

Jacksonville, founded as a gold-rush town in 1851, has been designated a National Historic District. Included among its restored buildings are the 1854 Methodist Church, the 1863 Beekman Bank, and the 1891 Rouge River Valley Railroad Depot.

Joaquin Miller's Cabin, in Canyon City, is the restored home of Oregon poet and writer Joaquin Miller.

McLoughlin House National Historic Site, in Oregon City, was built in 1845-46 by John McLoughlin, known as the Father of Oregon. Many of the house's original furnishings are still on display.

Methodist Mission Parsonage and Jason Lee Home, in Salem, are the restored buildings of the mission established by pioneer and missionary Jason Lee, founder of Willamette University.

Timberline Lodge, on Mount Hood, is a National Historic Landmark. Using local stone and timber, WPA workers built the lodge by hand in the late 1930s. The building, as well as its furnishings and interior ornamental artwork, have been carefully preserved.

The Pittock Mansion, in Portland, is the former home of Henry L. Pittock, founder of the newspaper that is now called the *Oregonian*. The French Renaissance-style structure, built from 1909 to 1914, included features unheard of at the time, such as modern showers and room-to-room telephones.

Other Interesting Places to Visit:

Bonneville Dam, the oldest major dam on the Columbia River, is one of Oregon's most popular attractions. At the visitor's center on Bradford Island, windows located below the surface of the water allow visitors to watch migrating salmon jump up fish ladders.

Columbia River Scenic Highway, in northern Oregon along the Columbia River, is a 24-mi. (39-km) scenic road offering spectacular views of the Columbia River Gorge. Highlights along the route include 720-ft. (219-m) Crown Point, a noted spot that affords a fantastic view of the gorge below; and 620-ft. (189-m) Multnomah Falls, one of the nation's highest waterfalls.

Crater Lake National Park, in southwest Oregon, is the site of Crater Lake, the nation's deepest lake. Formed about 6,600 years ago when a volcano collapsed, the lake is noted for its intensely blue color.

Hells Canyon, on the Oregon-Idaho border in northeast Oregon, is the deepest gorge in North America. The Hells Canyon National Recreation Area includes a 67-mi. (108-km) stretch of the Snake River that has been designated a National Wild and Scenic River.

John Day Fossil Beds National Monument, near John Day, is made up of three separate areas containing the fossilized bones of animals that lived in eastern Oregon as early as 30 million years ago. Exhibits at the visitor's center include the fossils of such long-extinct animals as three-toed horses, giant pigs, and saber-toothed cats.

Lava Lands, in the Deschutes National Forest near Bend, is a geological wonderland of volcanic formations. Highlights of the area include Lava Butte, a 500-ft. (152-m) cinder cone; Lava River Cave, a 1-mi.- (1.6-km-) long lava tube; and the world's largest forest of lava-cast trees.

Malheur National Wildlife Refuge, south of Burns, was established by President Theodore Roosevelt in 1908. More than 250 species of birds have been spotted in this 180,850-acre (73,188-hectare) refuge and nesting stop. A museum at the refuge headquarters displays more than two hundred mounted bird specimens.

Mount Hood, east of Portland, offers year-round skiing and countless other outdoor activities. Highways 26 and 35 together form the Mount Hood Loop, one of the Northwest's best-known scenic drives.

Oregon Caves National Monument, near Cave Junction, was popularized in the writings of Joaquin Miller as the "Marble Halls of Oregon." The site boasts such unusual limestone rock formations as Paradise Lost, The River Styx, Petrified Garden, and Banana Grove.

Oregon Coast, which stretches for 400 mi. (644 km) from Brookings to Astoria, is noted for its awesome beauty. Miles of sandy beaches, cliffs, coves, dunes, and more than fifty state parks offer visitors an immense variety of topography and wildlife.

IMPORTANT DATES

A.D. 1500s—The Chinooks, Clackamas, Kalapuyas, Multnomahs, Klamaths, Modocs, Paiutes, Cayuse, Rogues, Tillamooks, Nez Percé, and other Indian groups live in what is now Oregon

1542—Spanish explorer Bartolomé Ferrelo sails along the Oregon coast

1579—English explorer Sir Francis Drake sails past the Oregon coast

1728—Danish navigator Vitus Bering, sailing for Peter the Great of Russia, discovers the Bering Sea, extending Russian influence in the Oregon region as far south as what is now California

1774—Spanish explorer Juan Pérez searches for a "Northwest Passage"

1775—Spanish navigator Bruno Heceta discovers, but does not enter, the Columbia River

1788—John Kendrick and Robert Gray become the first American seamen to visit the Northwest Coast

1792—Robert Gray becomes the first white person to sail into the Columbia River, which he names for his ship; English Captain George Vancouver begins exploring the region

1805—Meriwether Lewis and William Clark spend the winter of 1805-06 at Fort Clatsop at the mouth of the Columbia River

1811—John Jacob Astor's Pacific Fur Company is established at Astoria

1813—Astor's Pacific Fur Company is sold to the British-owned North West Company

1818—A treaty between Britain and the United States provides for the joint occupation of Oregon

1819—The California-Oregon border is set at 42° N. by a treaty with Spain

1821 — The North West Company is sold to the Hudson's Bay Company, a British firm headed by John McLoughlin

1827 — The treaty between the United States and Britain providing for the joint occupation of Oregon is renewed

1834 — Jason Lee establishes a Methodist mission that becomes the first permanent American settlement in the Willamette Valley

1836 — Marcus Whitman and H.H. Spalding establish missions near present-day Walla Walla, Washington

1842 — Willamette University, the oldest university west of the Mississippi River, is founded

1843 — The first large migration of American settlers over the Oregon Trail arrives in Oregon; a provisional government is created by Americans living in the Willamette Valley

1846 — President James K. Polk signs a treaty with Britain that divides the Oregon Territory along the 49th Parallel

1847 — Marcus Whitman, his wife, and twelve others are massacred by Cayuse Indians near present-day Walla Walla

1848 — Congress establishes Oregon Territory

1849 — The first territorial legislature meets at Oregon City

1850 — Congress passes the Oregon Donation Land Law

1851 — Gold is discovered along Jackson Creek in southern Oregon; the Rogue River Indian War begins

1852 — The territorial capital is moved from Oregon City to Salem

1857 — Oregon's state constitution, still in effect today, is adopted

1859 — Oregon is admitted to the Union as the thirty-third state

1872 — The Modoc War is fought after the federal government tries to force Modoc Indians onto the Klamath reservation

1877 — The Nez Percé War is fought after the federal government tries to force Nez Percé Indians to move from their homeland in the Wallowa Valley to a reservation in Idaho

1883 — The Northern Pacific Railway reaches Portland

1893 — The state capitol at Salem is completed

1902 — Oregon adopts the initiative and referendum

1908 — Oregon adopts the recall

1911 — Reed College in Portland is established

1912 — Oregon women are granted the right to vote

1932 — Owyhee Dam is completed, bringing irrigation to the Owyhee and Snake river valleys

1933 — The Tillamook Burn (fire) wipes out 240,000 acres (97,126 hectares) of Oregon's finest timber

1935 — The capitol building is destroyed by fire

1937 — The Bonneville Dam is completed

1938 — Oregon voters pass by initiative one of the nation's first water-pollution-control laws; the new capitol building is opened at Salem

1947 — Oregon Governor Earl Snell, Oregon Secretary of State Robert S. Farrell, Jr., and Oregon President of the Senate Marshall Cornett are killed in an airplane crash

1951 — A state law calling for the control of air pollution goes into effect

1964 — Parts of western Oregon are damaged by heavy floods

1969 — The Department of Environmental Quality is established to enforce Oregon's environmental-protection laws

1973 — The state legislature enacts the nation's first law prohibiting the sale of nonreturnable beer and soft-drink containers

1980 — Mount St. Helens erupts, spewing ash over Portland and much of Oregon

1985 — Penny E. Harrington becomes the first woman to head the police force of a large American city when she is sworn in as police chief of Portland

1986 — President Reagan signs legislation creating a National Scenic Area along 85 mi. (137 km) of the Columbia River

1990 — Oregon begins an experiment in "rationing" health care in order to stretch state Medicaid funds; Barbara Roberts, Oregon's first woman governor, is elected

IMPORTANT PEOPLE

John Jacob Astor (1763-1848), fur trader, financier; organized the American Fur Company in 1808 to combat the British fur-trading monopoly in North America; organized the Pacific Fur Company in 1810 and established Astoria in 1811

Frederic Homer Balch (1861-1891), born in Lebanon; clergyman and writer; best known for *The Bridge of the Gods*, which was based on an Indian legend of a natural bridge that once crossed the Columbia River; other works include *Genevieve, A Tale of Oregon*, and *Memaloose*

BENJAMIN DE BONNEVILLE

Benjamin Louis Eulalie de Bonneville (1796-1878), soldier, explorer; arrived in Oregon in 1832 as part of a three-year exploration of the West; his expedition was the subject of American writer Washington Irving's 1837 book *The Adventures of Captain Bonneville*

Harold Lenoir Davis (1896-1960), born in Yoncalla; writer; specialized in stories of frontier life in the western and northwestern United States; won the 1936 Pulitzer Prize in fiction for *Honey in the Horn*; also wrote *Distant Music*, a chronicle of life on the Columbia River

PIERRE-JEAN DE SMET

Pierre-Jean De Smet (1801-1873), Jesuit missionary; worked among the Indians of the Northwest; known as "Blackrobe" by the Indians, who respected him for his honesty and fairness; was able to persuade the Sioux and other Indians to cease hostilities against whites and each other; founded St. Mary's Mission among the Flathead Indians in 1841

Richard Diebenkorn (1922-   ), artist; born in Portland; has received international acclaim for his abstract paintings

David Douglas (1798-1834), Scottish-born explorer and botanist; explored California, Oregon, and British Columbia (1823-24); the Douglas fir is named in his honor

DAVID DOUGLAS

Abigail Scott Duniway (1834-1915), teacher, author, publisher, and women's rights leader; helped found the Oregon State Woman Suffrage Association; published the weekly paper the *New Northwest*, which advocated women's rights; helped women gain the right to vote in Idaho, Washington, and Oregon

Eva Emery Dye (1855-1947), writer; forty-year resident of Oregon City; author of such historical novels as *McLoughlin and Old Oregon, The Conquest*, and *The True Story of Lewis and Clark*

John Charles Frémont (1813-1890), explorer, surveyor; explored much of the area between the Rocky Mountains and the Pacific Ocean; mapped the Oregon Trail during his first expedition to the Oregon country (1842)

EVA EMERY DYE

NEIL GOLDSCHMIDT

ROBERT GRAY

MARK HATFIELD

JASON LEE

Neil Goldschmidt (1940-   ), born in Eugene; politician, lawyer; mayor of Portland (1973-79); U.S. secretary of transportation under President Carter (1979-81); governor of Oregon (1987-91)

Robert Gray (1755-1806), fur trader, explorer; first American captain to sail around the world; established the basis for the U.S. claim to the Oregon country when he sailed the *Columbia* into what is now called the Columbia River (1792)

Mark O. Hatfield (1922-   ), born in Dallas; politician, educator; professor and dean of students at Willamette University (1950-56); state legislator (1951-57); Oregon secretary of state (1957-59); governor (1959-67); U.S. senator (1967-   ); as senator, has earned a national reputation as an independent, progressive Republican

Ernest Haycox (1899-1950), born in Portland; writer; author of more than twenty popular western-adventure novels; wrote the screenplays for a number of movies, including *Union Pacific, Apache Trail,* and *Stagecoach*

Ella Rhoads Higginson (1862-1940), poet; lived in La Grande; author of *When the Birds Go North Again, The Snowy Pearls,* and *The Vanishing Races and Other Poems*

Stewart H. Holbrook (1893-1964); editor, author, journalist; feature writer for the *Oregonian* (1930-37); his many books include *Holy Old Mackinaw, Ethan Allen,* and *Lost Men of American History*

Joseph (1840?-1904), born in the Wallowa Valley; Nez Percé chief; one of the leaders of the Nez Percé people during the Nez Percé War of 1877; helped lead his people on a 1,800-mi. (2,900-km) retreat toward Canada before surrendering to U.S. forces

Henry John Kaiser (1882-1967), industrialist; oversaw the construction of the Bonneville Dam on the Columbia River; during World War II his Portland shipyards produced a record number of "Liberty" ships and other vessels

Ken Kesey (1935-   ), writer; grew up in Springfield; best known for his novel *One Flew Over the Cuckoo's Nest*, the story of a sane man who is confined to a mental hospital, and *Sometimes a Great Notion*, about the lumber business

Joseph Lane (1801-1881), soldier, politician; first governor of Oregon Territory (1849-50); U.S. senator (1859-61); unsuccessful candidate for vice-president of the United States (1860)

Jason Lee (1803-1845), missionary, pioneer; came to the Oregon country in 1834 and established several Methodist missions over the next few years; in 1842 founded what is now called Willamette University, the first university west of the Mississippi; his statue represents Oregon in Statuary Hall in the U.S. Capitol

Asa Laurence Lovejoy (1808-1882), pioneer; helped found Portland; one of the authors of Oregon's state constitution; director of the East Side Oregon Central Railroad Company, the first railroad through the Willamette Valley

Bernard Malamud (1914-1988), writer, educator; taught at Oregon State University (1949-61); while living in Corvallis, wrote *The Natural*, *The Assistant*, *The Magic Barrel*, and *A New Life*, set in an Oregon college town

Edwin Markham (1852-1940), born Charles Edward Anson in Oregon City; poet, teacher; best-known poems are "The Man with the Hoe" and "Lincoln, the Man of the People"

EDWIN MARKHAM

Edison Marshall (1894-1967), writer; lived for many years in Medford, where he wrote such popular adventure stories as *The Voice of the Pack* and *The White Brigand*

Thomas Lawson McCall (1913-1983), radio and television journalist, politician; governor of Oregon (1967-75); noted for championing environmental-protection laws; as governor, cleaned up Oregon's rivers, made sure that stricter laws governing land use were adopted, and restricted private development of the Oregon coast

Phyllis McGinley (1905-1978), born in Ontario; teacher, poet, essayist; known for her wry and perceptive commentary on contemporary suburban life; frequent contributor to *The New Yorker*, *Vogue*, and other magazines; received the 1961 Pulitzer Prize in poetry for *Times Three: Selected Verse from Three Decades*

PHYLLIS McGINLEY

Douglas McKay (1893-1959), born in Salem, politician; mayor of Salem (1933-34); governor of Oregon (1949-52); U.S. secretary of the interior under President Eisenhower (1953-56)

John McLoughlin (1784-1857), physician, explorer, fur trader, and pioneer; generally considered the "Father of Oregon"; officer of the North West Company and the Hudson's Bay Company; controlled fur trading in the Northwest region; founded Oregon City (1842); assisted pioneers and missionaries settling in Oregon

CHARLES McNARY

Charles L. McNary (1874-1944), born near Salem, politician; U.S. senator (1917-44); Senate Majority Leader (1932-44); unsuccessful candidate for vice-president of the United States (1944)

Joseph Meek (1810-1875), trapper, pioneer, peace officer; U.S. marshall, Oregon Territory (1848-52); member of the legislature of Oregon's provisional government (1846-47); was sent as Oregon's representative to Washington, D.C., to seek government protection and territorial status following the 1847 Whitman Massacre

JOE MEEK

JOAQUIN MILLER

MAURINE NEUBERGER

LINUS PAULING

SYLVESTER PENNOYER

Cincinnatus Hiner (Joaquin) Miller (1837-1913), poet; as a boy, traveled from Indiana to Oregon and California; edited a newspaper in Eugene (1863); noted for his vivid, exaggerated accounts of life in the West; works include *Songs of the Sierras* and his autobiography, *Life Among the Modocs*

William Chadbourne (Chad) Mitchell (1936-   ), born in Portland; singer; leader of the Chad Mitchell Trio, which had several hit records in the 1960s and 1970s

Carl Morris (1911-   ), painter and educator; painted the mural *Port of Portland* for the Portland International Airport (1958); his works are exhibited in museums throughout the world

Wayne Lyman Morse (1900-1974), politician, educator; dean of the University of Oregon Law School (1931-34); U.S. senator (1945-69); leading opponent of the Vietnam War

Brent Woody Musburger (1939-   ), born in Portland; prominent television sportscaster

Richard Lewis Neuberger (1912-1960), born in Portland; writer, journalist, politician; Northwest correspondent for the *New York Times*, (1939-54); Oregon state representative (1941-42); Oregon state senator, (1949-54); U.S. senator (1955-60); author of *Our Promised Land, The Lewis and Clark Expedition,* and *Adventures in Politics*

Maurine Brown Neuberger (1907-   ), born in Cloverdale; teacher, writer, politician; taught in the Portland public schools (1929-45); Oregon state legislator (1951-55); elected a U.S. senator (1960-66) after a vacancy was left by the death of her husband, Senator Richard Neuberger

Robert (Bob) Packwood (1932-   ), born in Portland; lawyer, politician; Oregon state legislator (1963-69); U.S. senator (1969-   ); as the ranking Republican on the Senate Finance Committee, was influential in the passage of the Tax Reform Act of 1986; noted for his political independence and advocacy of women's rights

Francis Parkman (1823-1893), historian; made a 2,000-mi. (3,200-km), five-month trip to Oregon by horseback in 1846, during which he lived among the Indians, trappers, and hunters; his 1849 book *The California and Oregon Trail* (later published as simply *The Oregon Trail*) is an American classic that helped popularize the West

Linus Carl Pauling (1901-   ), born in Portland; chemist; received the 1954 Nobel Prize in chemistry for his work on chemical bonding; received the 1962 Nobel Peace Prize for his leadership in opposing the testing of nuclear weapons in the atmosphere

Sylvester Pennoyer (1831-1902), businessman, editor, politician; earned a fortune in the lumber and real-estate businesses; owner and editor of the *Oregon Herald*; mayor of Portland (1896-98); governor of Oregon (1887-95); as governor, supported the Populist cause and helped bring about political reform

John Reed (1887-1920), born in Portland, journalist, poet, revolutionary; won international fame for *Ten Days That Shook the World*, a sympathetic, eyewitness account of the 1917 Bolshevik Revolution in Russia

Mary Decker Slaney (1958-   ), professional runner; lives and trains in Eugene, where she has set five American and world records on the University of Oregon track; lost a chance for a gold medal in the 1984 Olympics when she was accidently tripped by another runner; also competed in the 1988 Olympics

MARY DECKER SLANEY

Eliza Hart Spalding (1807-1851), missionary, pioneer; she and Narcissa Whitman became the first white women to cross the Rockies and reach the Oregon Territory; with her husband, Reverend Henry Spalding, established a mission near present-day Lewiston, Idaho; worked with the Nez Percé Indians; escaped the Whitman Massacre in 1847; moved to the Willamette Valley

Thomas Nelson Strong (1853-1927), writer, lawyer; best known for *Cathlamet on the Columbia*, an account of frontier life and the influence of the forest and the area's Indians on the author's childhood and development

Richmond Kelley Turner (1885-1961), born in Portland; U.S. Navy admiral; principal architect of U.S. strategy in amphibious warfare during World War II; planned and led many important American assaults in the Pacific

RICHMOND TURNER

William Simon U'Ren (1859-1949), lawyer, political reformer; leading figure in Oregon's Progressive movement; organizer and secretary of the Oregon Direct Legislation League (1892-1902); as an Oregon state legislator (1897-98), worked to achieve direct voter participation in government; was instrumental in bringing the procedures of initiative, referendum, and recall to Oregon's governmental system

Frances Fuller Victor (1826-1902), poet, writer, historian; wrote the noted two-volume *History of Oregon* of Hubert Howe Bancroft's *History of the Pacific States*; other works include *The River of the West*, the *New Penelope, The Early Indian Wars of Oregon*, and *Poems*

WILLIAM U'REN

Henry Villard (1855-1900), German-born journalist and financier; newspaper reporter during the 1849 gold rush; helped complete the railroad linking Portland with California; organized the Oregon Railway and Navigation Company, which eventually linked Oregon with the East

Marcus Whitman (1802-1847), physician, pioneer, missionary; first visited Oregon in 1835; in 1836 established a mission among the Cayuse Indians near present-day Walla Walla, Washington; returned East in 1843; on his return trip, helped guide the first large party of American settlers to the Oregon Territory; was massacred, along with his wife Narcissa and twelve others, by Cayuse Indians in 1847

MARCUS WHITMAN

NARCISSA WHITMAN

Narcissa Prentiss Whitman (1808-1847), missionary, pioneer; one of the first two white women to cross the Rocky Mountains and reach the Oregon Territory; helped establish missions among the Cayuse Indians; was massacred by Cayuse Indians in 1847

Nathaniel Jarvis Wyeth (1802-1856), trader, explorer; built Fort William at the mouth of the Willamette River; leader of the 1834 expedition that brought Jason Lee to Oregon

GOVERNORS

John Whiteaker	1859-1862
Addison C. Gibbs	1862-1866
George L. Woods	1866-1870
LaFayette Grover	1870-1877
Stephen F. Chadwick	1877-1878
William W. Thayer	1878-1882
Zenas F. Moody	1882-1887
Sylvester Pennoyer	1887-1895
William Paine Lord	1895-1899
T. T. Geer	1899-1903
George E. Chamberlain	1903-1909
Frank W. Benson	1909-1910
Jay Bowerman	1910-1911
Oswald West	1911-1915
James Withycombe	1915-1919
Ben W. Olcott	1919-1923
Walter M. Pierce	1923-1927
Isaac Lee Patterson	1927-1929
Albin W. Norblad	1929-1931
Julius L. Meier	1931-1935
Charles H. Martin	1935-1939
Charles A. Sprague	1939-1943
Earl Snell	1943-1947
John H. Hall	1947-1949
Douglas McKay	1949-1952
Paul L. Patterson	1952-1956
Elmo E. Smith	1956-1957
Robert D. Holmes	1957-1959
Mark O. Hatfield	1959-1967
Thomas L. McCall	1967-1975
Robert W. Straub	1975-1979
Victor G. Atiyeh	1979-1987
Neil Goldschmidt	1987-1991
Barbara Roberts	1991-

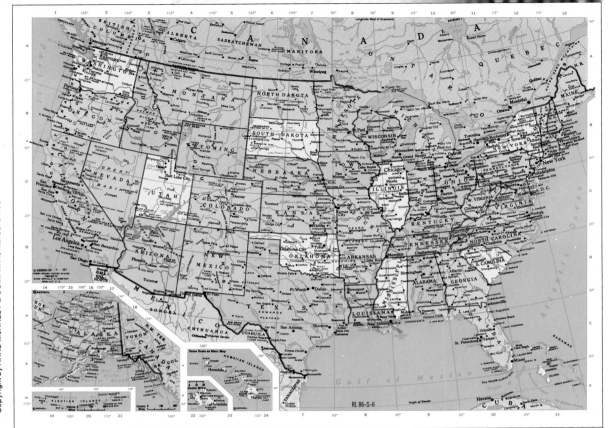

Topography

MAP KEY

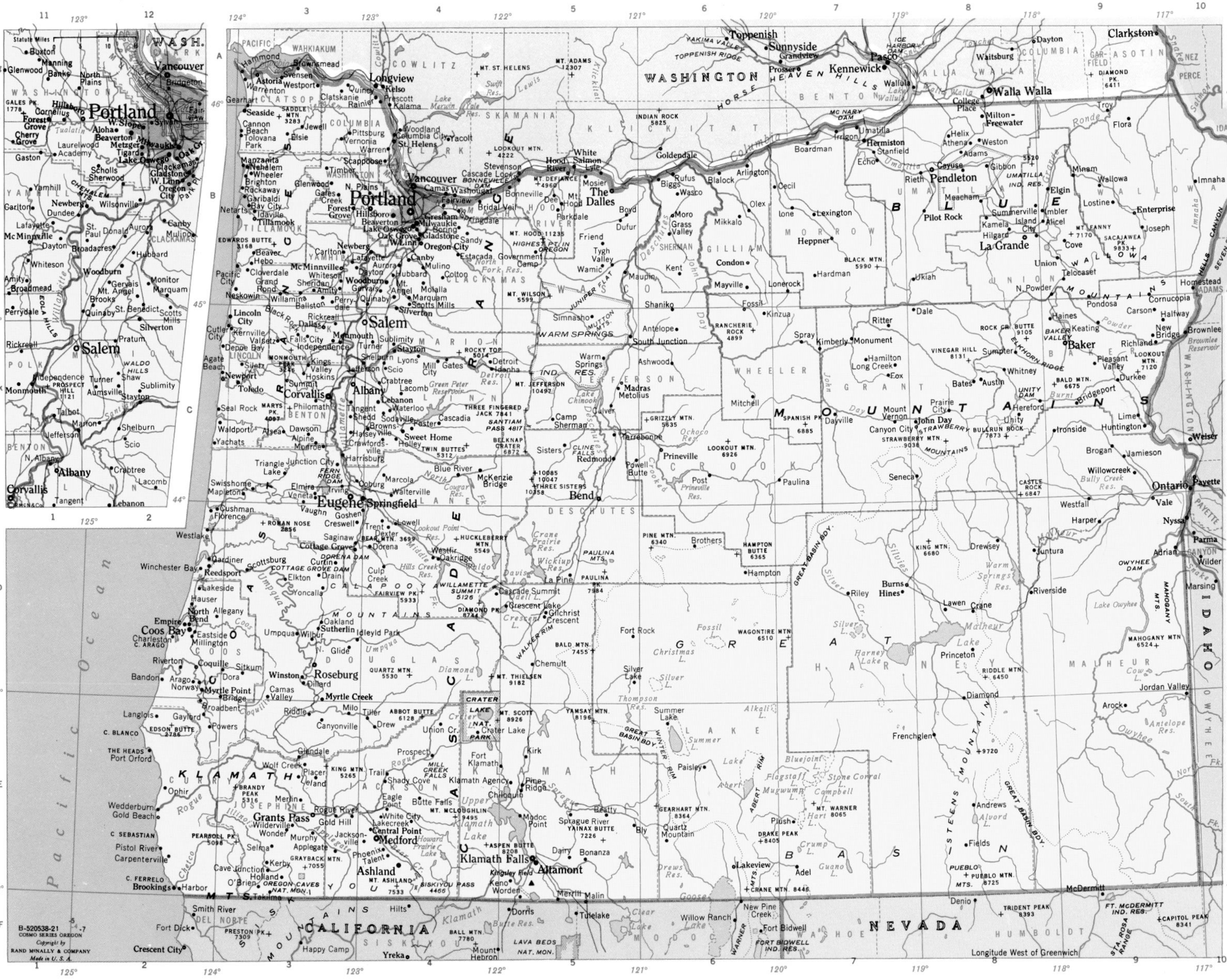
WASHINGTON
IDAHO
NEVADA
CALIFORNIA
Pacific Ocean
Portland
Salem
Eugene
Springfield
Corvallis
Albany
Medford
Klamath Falls
Bend
Pendleton
La Grande
Baker
Ontario
Coos Bay
Roseburg
Grants Pass
Ashland
The Dalles
Vancouver
Walla Walla
Kennewick
Pasco
Longview
Clarkston
Lakeview
Burns
John Day
Astoria
Crescent City
Yreka
Longitude West of Greenwich
B-520538-21
COSMO SERIES OREGON
Copyright by
RAND McNALLY & COMPANY
Made in U.S.A.

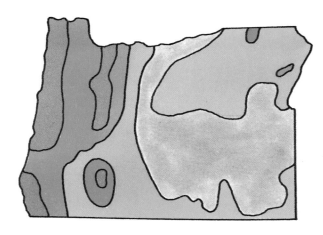

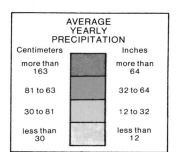

AVERAGE YEARLY PRECIPITATION

Centimeters		Inches
more than 163		more than 64
81 to 63		32 to 64
30 to 81		12 to 32
less than 30		less than 12

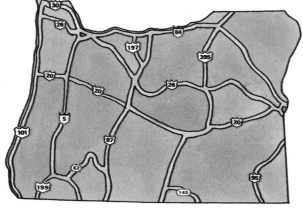

MAJOR HIGHWAYS

FOREST PRODUCTS   BEEF   BARLEY
DAIRY PRODUCTS   POULTRY   SUGAR BEETS
HOGS   MINING   BEANS
NURSERY PRODUCTS   POTATOES   BERRIES
FISH   WHEAT   OATS
MANUFACTURING   HAY   GRASS SEED
SHEEP   VEGETABLES   HOPS
WALNUTS   FRUIT   MINT
                                     CRANBERRIES

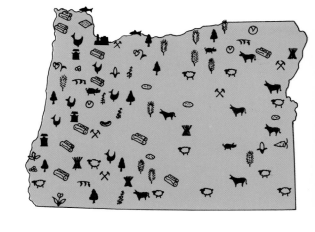

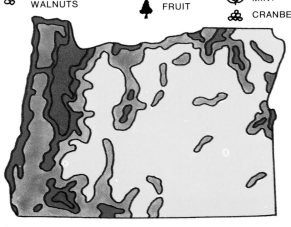

POPULATION DENSITY

Number of persons per square kilometer		Number of persons per square mile
more than 20		more than 50
10 to 20		25 to 50
4 to 10		10 to 25
less than 4		less than 10

TOPOGRAPHY

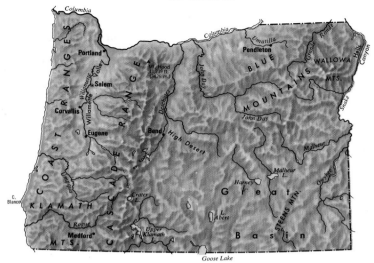

Columbia
Columbia
Umatilla
Pendleton
Portland
BLUE
Grande Ronde
WALLOWA
MTS.
Salem
Mt. Hood
11,239 ft.
(3426 m.)
John Day
MOUNTAINS
Hells Canyon
Corvallis
Willamette Valley
Deschutes
John Day
Snake
Eugene
Bend
High Desert
Malheur
C. Blanco
Umpqua
Malheur L.
Owyhee
Harney
Great
Crater L.
Malheur
L.
Rogue
KLAMATH
CASCADE RANGE
STEENS MTN.
COAST RANGES
Upper Klamath
L. Abert
Medford
MTS.
Basin

Goose Lake

Courtesy of Hammond, Incorporated
Maplewood, New Jersey

| Below Sea Level | 100 m. 328 ft. | 200 m. 656 ft. | 500 m. 1,640 ft. | 1,000 m. 3,281 ft. | 2,000 m. 6,562 ft. | 5,000 m. 16,404 ft. |

COUNTIES

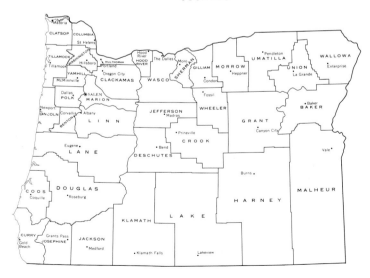

Astoria
CLATSOP
COLUMBIA
St Helens
Hood River
The Dalles
Moro
WALLOWA
TILLAMOOK
Pendleton
UMATILLA
Tillamook
Washington
Hillsboro
MULTNOMAH
Portland
HOOD RIVER
GILLIAM
MORROW
UNION
Enterprise
YAMHILL
Oregon City
Heppner
La Grande
McMinnville
CLACKAMAS
WASCO
SHERMAN
Condon
Dallas
POLK
SALEM
MARION
Fossil
Newport
Corvallis
Albany
JEFFERSON
Madras
WHEELER
Baker
BAKER
LINCOLN
BENTON
LINN
GRANT
Canyon City
Eugene
LANE
Prineville
CROOK
Vale
Bend
DESCHUTES
COOS
DOUGLAS
Coquille
Roseburg
Burns
HARNEY
MALHEUR
CURRY
Gold Beach
Grants Pass
JOSEPHINE
JACKSON
KLAMATH
LAKE
Medford
Klamath Falls
Lakeview

A rural scene in Wallowa County in northeastern Oregon

INDEX

Page numbers that appear in boldface type indicate illustrations

A sheepherder on Steens Mountain in southeastern Oregon

Picture Identifications
Front Cover: Highway 101 and rock formations south of Cape Sebastian
Back Cover: Mount Hood
Pages 2-3: Vista House at sunrise, Columbia River Gorge
Page 6: Bridal Veil Creek
Pages 8-9: Crown Point in the Columbia River Gorge
Pages 22-23: Montage of Oregon residents
Page 28: Detail of *Falls at Colville*, an 1848 painting by Paul Kane
Pages 38-39: *The Oregon Trail*, an 1869 painting by Albert Bierstadt
Page 52: An Oregon train in the late 1800s
Page 64: Pear orchards in the Hood River Valley
Pages 76-77: Nighttime festivities during the 1987 Portland Rose Festival
Pages 88-89: Botanical Gardens at Shore Acres State Park
Page 108: Montage showing the state flag, the state tree (Douglas fir), the state bird (western meadowlark), the state animal (beaver), and the state flower (Oregon grape)

Picture Acknowledgments

© **Steve Terrill:** Front cover, Back cover, 2-3, 4, 6, 8-9, 11, 12 (top left, bottom left), 13 (bottom left, right), 14 (left, top right), 15 (top left, bottom left), 16, 18, 19, 20, 22 (middle left), 23 (top right, bottom right), 66, 68 (right), 69, 71 (left), 74, 75, 80, 88-89, 92, 94, 95 (left), 96, 98, 99 (right), 102 (left), 103 (left), 105, 106, 108 (Douglas firs), 112, 113, 114, 119, 121, 138, 141
Root Resources: © D.C. Lowe: 5, 13 (top left), 70, 83 (bottom left); © Max Gutierrez: 17 (left), 22 (bottom right); © E. Simms: 68 (left); © Anthony Mercieca: 108 (meadowlark)
R/C Photo Agency: © Earl L. Kubis: 14 (bottom right), 22 (top right), 71 (right); © Betty A. Kubis: 15 (right)
© **Larry Geddis:** 17 (right), 76-77, 79, 83 (right), 86, 99 (left), 104, 115, 122
C-III Sports: © R.M. Collins III: 22 (middle right), 84
TSW-Click/Chicago Ltd.: © James P. Rowan: 22 (bottom left), © Jose Carrillo: 23 (top left)
Shostal Associates: 64; © George and Monserrate Schwartz: 23 (bottom left)
Tom Stack & Associates: © F. Stuart Westmorland: 25; © Scott Blackman: 72
Royal Ontario Museum: 28, 31
Oregon Historical Society: 32, 36 (inset), 43 (bottom), 46, 49, 55, 59, 61, 128 (Lee), 130 (Pennoyer), 131 (U'Ren), 132
The Granger Collection: 35, 56, 82 (left), 127 (Bonneville, Douglas), 129 (Markham, McGinley), 130 (Miller)
Amon Carter Museum, Fort Worth, Texas: 36
Butler Institute of American Art: 38-39
Historical Pictures Service, Inc., Chicago: 43 (top), 127 (De Smet), 128 (Gray), 129 (McNary), 130 (Pauling), 131 (Whitman)
Smithsonian Institution: 50 (left)
National Park Service: 50 (right)
The Bettmann Archive: 52
Wide World Photos: 82 (right), 128 (Goldschmidt, Hatfield), 130 (Neuberger), 131 (Slaney, Turner)
© **John Giustina:** 83 (top left)
The Oregonian, © **Brent Wojahn:** 85
Photri: 107, 117; © Biedel: 87, 93; © R. Atkeson: 101, 103 (right)
© **Bob and Ira Spring:** 91, 102 (right)
© **Lynn M. Stone:** 95 (right)
©**Reinhard Brucker:** 108 (Oregon grape flower)
Gartman Agency: © Christy Volpe: 108 (beaver)
Third Coast Stock Source: © Ed Kreminski: 118
Oregon Symphony: 120
North Wind Picture Archives: 127 (Dye)
Montana Historical Society: 129 (Meek)
Courtesy Flag Research Center, Winchester, Massachusetts: Flag on 108
Len W. Meents: Maps on 91, 93, 96, 101, 106, 136

About the Author

R. Conrad Stein was born and grew up in Chicago. He began writing professionally shortly after graduating from the University of Illinois. He is the author of many books, articles, and short stories written for young readers. To prepare for this book, Mr. Stein traveled extensively in Oregon, where he was awed by the marvelous scenery and charmed by the friendly people. Mr. Stein lives in Chicago with his wife and their daughter Janna.